CANADA'S AGING POPULATION

by

Susan A. McDaniel
University of Waterloo

Butterworths
Toronto and Vancouver

Canada's Aging Population
© 1986 Butterworths, A division of Reed Inc.

All rights reserved. No part of this publication may be reproduced, stored in a retrieval system, or transmitted, in any form or by any means (photocopying, electronic, mechanical, recording, or otherwise), without the prior written permission of the copyright holder.

Printed and bound in Canada by John Deyell Company

The Butterworth Group of Companies
Canada
Butterworths, Toronto and Vancouver
United Kingdom
Butterworth & Co. (Publishers) Ltd., London and Edinburgh
Australia
Butterworth Pty Ltd., Sydney, Melbourne, Brisbane, Adelaide and Perth
New Zealand
Butterworths (New Zealand) Ltd., Wellington and Auckland
Singapore
Butterworth & Co. (Asia) Pte. Ltd., Singapore
South Africa
Butterworth Publishers (SA) (Pty) Ltd., Durban and Pretoria
United States
Butterworth Legal Publishers, Boston, Seattle, Austin and St. Paul
D&S Publishers, Clearwater

Canadian Cataloguing in Publication Data

McDaniel, Susan A., 1946-
  Canada's aging population

(Perspectives on individual and population aging)
Bibliography: p.
Includes index.
ISBN 0-409-84913-8

1. Aged – Social aspects – Canada. 2. Canada – Population. 3. Aged – Government policy – Canada. I. Title. II. Series.

HQ1064.C3M23   1986   305.2'6'0971   C86-093301-6

Sponsoring Editor: Janet Turner
Managing Editor: Linda Kee
Supervisory Editor: Marie Graham
Editor: Kathleen Hamilton
Cover Design: Patrick Ng
Production: Jim Shepherd

For Lola Anderson and Frank Anderson,
who never had the opportunity
to enjoy old age.

BUTTERWORTHS PERSPECTIVES ON INDIVIDUAL AND POPULATION AGING SERIES

The initiation of this Series represents an exciting and significant development for gerontology in Canada. Since the production of Canadian-based knowledge about individual and population aging is expanding rapidly, students, scholars and practitioners are seeking comprehensive yet succinct summaries of the literature on specific topics. Recognizing the common need of this diverse community of gerontologists, Janet Turner, Sponsoring Editor at Butterworths, conceived the idea of a series of specialized monographs that could be used in gerontology courses to complement existing texts and, at the same time, to serve as a valuable reference for those initiating research, developing policies, or providing services to elderly Canadians.

Each monograph includes a state-of-the-art review and analysis of the Canadian-based scientific and professional knowledge on the topic. Where appropriate for comparative purposes, information from other countries is introduced. In addition, some important policy and program implications of the current knowledge base are discussed, and unanswered policy and research questions are raised to stimulate further work in the area. The monographs have been written for a wide audience: undergraduate students in a variety of gerontology courses; graduate students and research personnel who need a summary and analysis of the Canadian literature prior to initiating research projects; practitioners who are involved in the daily planning and delivery of services to aging adults; and policy-makers who require current and reliable information in order to design, implement and evaluate policies and legislation for an aging population.

The decision to publish a monograph on a specific topic has been based in part on the relevance of the topic for the academic and professional community, as well as on the extent of information available at the time an author is signed to a contract. Thus, not all the conceivable topics are included in the early stages of the Series and some topics are published earlier rather than later. Because gerontology in Canada is attracting large numbers of highly qualified graduate students as well as increasingly active research personnel in academic, public and private settings, new areas of concentrated research will evolve. Hence, additional monographs that review and analyze work in these areas will be needed to reflect the evolution of knowledge on specialized topics pertaining to individual or population aging in Canada.

Before introducing the first monograph in the Series, I would like, on behalf of the Series' authors and the gerontology community, to acknowledge the following members of the Butterworths "team" and their respective staffs for their unique and sincere contribution to gerontology in Canada: Geoffrey Burn, President, for his continuing support of the project despite difficult times in the Canadian publishing industry; Janet Turner, Sponsoring Editor, for her vision, endurance and high academic standards; Linda Kee, Managing Editor, for her coordination of the production, especially her constant reminders to authors (and the Series Editor) that the hands of the clock continue to move in spite of our perceptions that manuscript deadlines were still months or years away; Jim Shepherd, Production Manager, for nimbly vaulting many a technical obstacle; and Gloria Vitale, Academic Sales Manager, for her support and promotion of the Series. For each of you, we hope the knowledge provided in this Series will have personal value — but not until well into the next century!

Barry D. McPherson

FOREWORD

This first monograph in the Butterworths Series, *Perspectives on Individual and Population Aging*, presents a comprehensive and unique analysis of the causes and consequences of population aging in Canada. As a social demographer with expertise on the issues of women, health and aging, Professor McDaniel introduces interesting linkages between demographic processes and a number of biological, psychological and sociological processes that can have an impact on both aging individuals and aging populations. This monograph is not a simple, descriptive "fact book" about the demographic characteristics of older Canadians. Rather, the author describes and develops, in depth, alternative explanations and interpretations of demographic patterns and issues related to population aging in Canada. Of particular significance is her scholarly effort to dispel the myths surrounding population aging. Furthermore, in keeping with the goals of the first monograph in a series, the reader is introduced to a number of questions and issues that will be discussed more completely in later monographs: housing, institutionalization, the family, women, ethnicity, migration, health care, crime, retirement and widowhood.

In summary, this monograph provides the reader — whether practitioner, policy-maker, researcher, volunteer, or student in a gerontology or demography course — with an interesting, useful and comprehensive review and analysis of how and why population aging has occurred. In addition, we learn how demographic information can be used to more competently develop policies and provide services that will meet the present and future needs of older Canadians. I urge you to seriously think about and discuss the implications of the ideas introduced in this monograph, the foundation of the Series.

Barry D. McPherson, Ph.D.
Series Editor
Waterloo, Ontario, Canada
March 1986

PREFACE

The study of aging is a "growth industry" at present in Canada and throughout the Western industrialized world. One reason for the recent increased attention to aging is the growing relative importance of older people, both economically and politically. Still another reason, and perhaps the most important from the point of view of this book, is the need to plan for societies that are growing older demographically. Relatively little is known about the processes of individual and societal aging, or about the middle and later stages of the life cycle, while much is known about the early stages. Aging is a complex process involving biological, psychological, social, political and economic factors. Partly because of this complexity, aging is poorly understood, and until recently it has not been accorded much priority as an important process to be studied.

Whatever the reasons, this recent attention to the aging process is welcome. There is an enormous need for new research on aging. There is also a need to synthesize the existing research. With this knowledge, we will be better prepared to develop well-informed plans for the future and to address the as yet unanswered questions about the aging process.

In this first book in the Aging Series, the focus is on Canada's aging population. One possible approach to examining the process of population aging is by means of statistical tables, graphs and data. Several books of this type have already been written, including: the Health and Welfare Canada (1982) report, *Canadian Governmental Report on Aging*, and the Health and Welfare Canada (1983) report, *Fact Book on Aging in Canada*. Both are highly recommended for those who are interested in more data.

While crucially important, a mass of statistical data can be confusing. It can also be distracting to the person who wants to know about the social issues associated with an aging population. This book is intended to be more than descriptive. In fact, a deliberate attempt has been made here to keep tables, graphs and charts to a minimum. The emphasis is on identification and interpretation of social patterns and issues involved in population aging in Canada. A minimal number of carefully selected tables and graphs are provided as illustrations.

Demographic or population aging is the process whereby an entire population grows older. The future pattern of having children, known in demography as fertility, is the single most important variable in population aging, as will be shown in the chapters that follow. Not-yet-born Canadians play a central role in demographic aging. Thus you must consider not only your own age group's retirement, in order to comprehend demographic aging, you must also consider the childbearing patterns of your generation and those that follow.

Population aging does not occur in a vacuum or in a computer. It occurs within a social and economic context. Although conceptually, demographic aging is not the same as individual aging, linkages have been made between the biological and psychological processes of individual aging and the demographic process. Many of these attempts at drawing links are informative and fruitful. Others, unfortunately, are far-fetched and not well based in fact. Similar remarks can be made about the links between demographic aging and the social or economic structure. One aim of this book is to begin to sort out the valid thought and research on demographic aging from the less well conceived research and theory. This book is thus a critique of the "state of the art," as well as a synthesis and interpretation of existing research and theory on demographic aging in Canada.

Population aging, as may be evident from the discussion so far, is a process with implications in many fields, including the social, economic, psychological, health-related, planning-related, political and philosophical. A wide range of disciplines and viewpoints are involved, bringing interest and complexity to the study of population aging, as well as the inevitable territorial battles.

Those who frame social policy often look to social science research, theory and debate for guidance. A major aim of this book is to explore central policy issues associated with demographic aging, and to provoke discussion on these issues.

The book begins with an exploration of the nature and causes of demographic aging (Chapter 1). A critical comparison is made of the basic measures of demographic aging. Chapter 2 examines the perspectives from which population aging is analyzed by researchers. The Canadian experience, both historical and present-day, is discussed in Chapter 3. Comparisons with the world situation are also made. In Chapter 4, selected contemporary concerns related to population aging are discussed, including zero population growth, economic issues, mobility and women's problems in an aging society. Chapter 5 focuses on policy and program implications of population aging, including economic policies, work issues, health, quality of life, and home and educational policies. In Chapter 6, the future of demographic aging in Canada is anticipated. Speculation is offered about future trends in fertility, mortality and immigration, as well as the future age structure of Canadian society. In the last chapter (Chapter 7) the implications of demographic aging are discussed and some as yet unanswered research questions raised.

ACKNOWLEDGEMENTS

Being the author of the first book in a series is both an honour and an obligation, for it means leading the way for the series, and setting the pace and tone for the books that will follow. As well, the first book in a new series is often researched and written over the shortest period of time, so that it can indeed be the first one published. This places another type of obligation on the author.

Given the heavy pressures of high standards and time, the author is much indebted to the many friends and colleagues who provided generous help and support throughout the writing of the book. They are too numerous to all be named. Special thanks are extended to Barry McPherson, the Series Editor, whose expert editing and advice made for a much improved final version. Thanks also to Janet Turner, Linda Kee and the other editors at Butterworths for their patience, expertise and unstinting support. Carl Grindstaff of the University of Western Ontario is to be specially thanked for reading the manuscript and providing excellent comments on short notice. Thanks to Anatole Romaniuc and M. V. George of the Demography Division, Statistics Canada for providing me with data, both published and unpublished.

The students on whom many of these ideas were first tested deserve thanks for their enthusiastic response. Graduate students who tolerated short meetings and fast passings in the hallways are also thanked for their understanding. Thank you to Bill Forbes of Gerontology at Waterloo for his help and support as well as the opportunity to try these ideas on the students in his gerontology seminar. Very special thanks to Bev Taylor for her friendly patience in typing the manuscript and making revision after revision while the pressured author pushed. Thanks also to Ursula Ortmann and Julie Dembski for their helpful assistance. Thanks to my Department Chairman, Dan Kubat, for providing computer time and department funds for typing the manuscript. Thank you is insufficient to express my gratitude to my special friend, Doug, for providing inspiration and part of the incentive to work so hard. My many friends who endured my absence, even when I was physically present, at social occasions during the summer of 1985 are appreciated for their continuing loyalty and support. I am much indebted to many, but the ultimate responsibility for anything said in the book is mine.

S. A. McDaniel, Ph.D.
Department of Sociology
University of Waterloo

CONTENTS

Butterworths Perspectives on Individual and Population Aging Series v
Foreword vii
Preface ix
Acknowledgements xi
List of Tables xvii
List of Figures xix

Chapter 1: Population Aging: Causes, Myths and Measures 1

    Demographic Aging: What Is It? 2
        Demographic Aging and Age Structure 3
        Age Dynamics and Cohort Flow 3
    Causes of Demographic Aging 5
        Factors Contributing to Population Aging 5
        The Demographic Transition and Population Aging 8
    Measures of Demographic Aging 9
        Proportion of Elderly People in the Population 10
        Dependency Ratios and Old/Young Ratios 11
        Median Age 13
        Years Remaining until Death 13
        Disability-free Life Expectancy 14
        The Slope of the Population Pyramid 15
    Conclusion 15

Chapter 2: Perspectives on Population Aging: Conceptual
             and Research Approaches 19

    The Power of Perspective 19
    Central Approaches to Population Aging 22
        The Demographic Descriptive Approach 23
        The Structural Approaches 24
            Demographic Determinism 25
            The Crisis Approach 26
            The Contextual Approach 27
    Conclusion 28

Chapter 3: Demographic Aging: The Canadian Experience in
             World Context 29

Demographic Aging in World Context 29
    Sex and Age Groups in World Aging 30
Demographic Aging in Canada: Past and Present 35
    Aging in Canada's Past 36
    Contemporary Aging Patterns in Canada 40
        Sex Ratio 40
        Place of Residence 41
        Language and Ethnicity 42
        Size of the Older Population 43
Conclusion 43

Chapter 4: Contemporary Issues and Concerns about Population Aging 45

The Advent of Zero Population Growth 45
    Zero Population Growth and Mortality 46
    The Link between Population Growth and Economic Growth 47
    Aging, Zero Population Growth, and Level of Economic Development 49
    Changing Attitudes toward Population in the Advent of Zero Growth 51
Economic Concerns in an Aging Population 53
    Shifting Economic and Demographic Dependency Burdens .. 53
    Productivity and Creativity Concerns 56
    Wealth Distribution 58
Mobility and Opportunity Structure in an Aging Population 59
    The Age Structure Argument 60
    Population Aging and Mobility 61
The Particular Problems of Women in an Aging Society 63
    The Predominance of Older Women 63
    The Confusion of Women's Dependency with Population Aging 65
Conclusion 65

Chapter 5: Policy and Program Implications of Population Aging .. 67

Economic Issues 68
    Economic Dependency and Pensions 68
    Economic Problems of Older Women 70
    Economic Growth and Productivity 73
Retirement and Work Issues 75
    The Growing Number of Retirees 76
    The Changing Meaning of Work 77
    Policy Implications of Volunteer Work 79

Health Issues 79
  General Policy Concerns of Health Care in Canada 80
  Myths and Misconceptions about Aging and Health 81
  Health Care Provision 82
  Health Care Costs 84
  Quality of Life 85
Housing and Family Issues 86
  The Changing Canadian Family 87
  Housing and Home Care 88
Education Issues 90
Conclusion 92

Chapter 6: The Future of Demographic Aging 93

Future Canadian Trends in Fertility, Mortality and Immigration . 93
  The Future of Fertility 94
  The Future of Mortality 98
  The Future of International Migration 99
Canada's Age Structure in the Future 101
  Implications of Canada's Present Age-Sex Structure 102
  Canada's Future Age-Sex Structure 104
  Canada's Future Age Group Relationships 111
Conclusion 114

Chapter 7: Implications of Demographic Aging and Unanswered Research Questions 115

Summary 115
Implications of Demographic Aging for Canada 117
Unanswered Questions 118
Conclusion 120

Bibliography 121

TABLES

1.1	Relative Effects on Aging of Mortality and Fertility Declines	9
3.1	Percentages of Population Aged 65 and over, by Sex, for Major Regions of the World, 1980	30
3.2	Percentage Distribution of the Population, by Three Age Groups, for Selected Industralized Countries, early 1980s	32
3.3	Old-Age Dependency Ratios for Selected Countries, 1950 to 1980, and Projected to 2025	33
3.4	Three Measures of Demographic Aging for Canada, 1851 to 1981	36
3.5	Labour Force Age Composition in Canada, 1851 to 1981	40
6.1	Percentage of Population 65 Years and Over Canada, 1981, and Projected to 2031 (Low- and High-Growth Scenarios)	106
6.2	Percentage of Population in Working Ages for Canada, 1981, and Projected to 2031 (Low- and High-Growth Scenarios)	107
6.3	Percentage of the Population 65 Years and Over for Canada and Provinces, 1981, 1991, 2006 (Low-Growth Scenario)	110
6.4	Total Dependency Ratios (Total Population /20-64) for Canada, 1976, 1981 and Projected to 2051 (Old and Young Population Projections)	112
6.5	Youth, Old Age and Total Dependency Ratios for Canada, 1971, 1981, and Projected to 2031 (Low-Growth Scenario)	113

FIGURES

1.1	Population Pyramids, Canada, 1881 and 1976	7
1.2	Least Squares Line Applied to Canada, 1901, 1951, and Projected to 2001	16
3.1	Historical and Future Age Composition, Canada, 1851 to 2051	38
3.2	Partial Age Pyramids for the Population Aged 65 and Over, Canada, 1961, 1981, 2001 and 2021	42
6.1	Populations by Age and Sex, Canada, 1981, Projected to 2006 and 2031 (Low-Growth Scenario)	95
6.2	Percentages of Total Population in Selected Age Groups, Canada, 1951 to 2021	108
6.3	Ratios of Females to Males in Selected Age Groups, Canada, 1951 to 2001	109

CHAPTER 1

POPULATION AGING: CAUSES, MYTHS AND MEASURES

Demography is the study of populations. Demographic or population aging is the process whereby an entire population grows older. This process may be measured and conceptualized in a variety of ways. Most people think of aging on an individual level, and may have difficulty at first imagining how a population ages. Demographic aging indeed occurs on a different level of abstraction than individual aging. The concept of demographic aging, however, can be a useful tool by which to understand and explain changes in society, and a basis on which to develop policies and programs.

In order to think demographically, imagine yourself as a member of a particular age group within society; for example, you were born in 1966. In Canada today, on average, if you add 20 to 25 years to your birth date, you have the approximate year in which you will be in the labour force full-time. For women, adding 35 years to your birth date will show the year by which your childbearing (if you have children) will be complete or nearly complete. Adding 60 or 65 or even 70 years to your birth date will give you the year in which you will likely retire from the labour force.

For most of us, it is difficult to imagine what the world will be like in the year of our retirement. What is important to keep in mind when thinking about demographic or population aging is that people who will retire in Canada in 2031 are already born. They were born in 1966 and are now in their early years of working or are attending college or university. Of course, other people may become part of the Canadian population, through immigration, between now and 2031. Others will depart from Canada for other countries. Still others, unfortunately, will die before they reach retirement. Demographers know what the probabilities of these events will be, on the basis of past trends and current information. This, of course, does not mean that demographers can predict the probability of any given *individual* emigrating or dying, but *general* rates are known and projections can be made of the future population of Canada.

Population aging is a much discussed topic in modern industrial nations. In the rush to discover the social and economic implications of living in and planning for an aging society, many myths and misconceptions have been publicized in the media. In part, these misunderstandings stem from fear and alarmism. However, misconceptions also result from lack of understanding of the nature and causes of demographic aging, how it historically came to be, and its links with social and economic forces.

This chapter addresses some of the more common problems associated with understanding the process of population aging. It discusses what population aging actually is, and how it differs from the process of individual aging. The causes of population aging, with particular reference to the Canadian situation, are explored and some myths are dispelled. The basic measures of demographic aging are compared and contrasted, not simply as a descriptive "laundry list" but as part of the attempt to understand better what demographic aging means.

DEMOGRAPHIC AGING: WHAT IS IT?

Everyone has an idea of what aging means. To most people, the first idea that comes to mind is the gradual process of getting older, as revealed by greying hair, declining physical capacities or transition to grandparenthood. Aging might also mean the attainment of privileges, such as being able to borrow the family car, or being able to drink legally. All of these are part of the process of individual aging. Social aging, on the other hand, is the socio-cultural construction of age categories. For example, adolescents in our society are considered to be still in need of adult guidance, rather than being accepted as full adults as they are in many parts of the world. Similarly, older members of Canadian society do not command, for the most part, the kind of respect they do in many societies. For both the individual and society, aging means not only entry into old age, but biological and social progression from one stage to another throughout the life cycle.

When students are asked for the first time to think about population or demographic aging, they often get puzzled looks on their faces; they attempt to picture an entire society aging in terms of individual or social maturation. However, the terms of individual aging are quite inapplicable to the process of demographic aging. In fact, thinking in individual, biological terms can be quite misleading when dealing with the aging of populations.

To the general public, population aging most often means the process whereby a population is made up increasingly of older age groups, especially those 65 years and above. This view is supported by the United Nations' definition: a population is considered "aged" when more than 7 percent of it is over 65. While this definition is a commonly used index of population aging, the proportion of the population aged 65 or over is not the only, or even the most important, aspect of population aging. As Myles and Boyd (1982, 259) suggest, "... to say that a nation's population structure is aging is to say very little about either the absolute or the relative numbers of elderly persons to be found in that society at a particular point in time."

Demographic Aging and Age Structure

Population or demographic aging, like individual aging, involves changes at all ages, not simply those that occur at the older ages. It is a dynamic process that occurs over time, much like the process of individual aging. What is crucial in ascertaining the degree to which a population is aging, or whether it is, is not simply whether there is an increase in the population over the age of 65, but whether declines have occurred in the younger age groups, relative to those in the middle-aged categories.

To illustrate, during the decade of the 1970s Canada experienced a dramatic growth of 35.3 percent in the proportion of its population over the age of 65 (Statistics Canada 1984d, 1). By 1981, people 65 and over comprised 9.7 percent of the population, compared to 8.1 percent in 1971. In 1901, the figure was 5 percent (Myles and Boyd 1982, 261). However, despite its obvious and dramatic expansion, the older population was not the fastest growing group in Canada in the 1970s. In fact, the age group 20-34 increased 37.3 percent during this decade, reflecting the entry to adulthood of the large baby boom generation (Statistics Canada 1984d, 1). At the same time, while these dramatic increases were occurring among younger adults and older Canadians, the proportion of the population 5-14 years old declined 19 percent. Thus, Canada experienced demographic aging during the 1970s not only because the older population grew, relative to the total population, but also because the younger population decreased, relative to the middle-aged population.

This contraction of the younger population may be as important in the process of demographic aging as the growth in the older population. To focus only on expansion of the older population would be misleading, because important components of the process of demographic aging occurring at other ages would be overlooked. The degree to which demographic aging is occurring could be underestimated. The concept of demographic aging is a relative one that reflects changes occurring throughout the age structure.

Despite the impressive growth in the proportion of Canada's older population in one decade, the 1970s, and the fact that Canada would qualify as an aged country according to the United Nations, the proportion of Canada's population that is elderly is actually low in comparison to most other industrial countries of the world (Statistics Canada, 1984a, 40). This will be discussed in detail in Chapter 3. Canada, by international comparison, ranks among the least aged countries in the industrialized world, even though we have been experiencing demographic aging for over a century. Thus, demographic aging and what constitutes an aged population are relative.

Age Dynamics and Cohort Flow

Central to the understanding of demographic aging are the concepts of age dynamics and cohort flow. Both concepts have recently caught the public attention. Although part of the demographers' "tool box" for years, they were introduced to the public in 1978 with the presidential address of Richard Easterlin to the Population Association of America (Easterlin 1978). A popularized account of this address appeared in *Psychology Today* in 1979 (Collins 1979) with subsequent commentaries in *The New York Times* and *The Wall Street Journal*. This is attention not often given to demography, once termed the "dismal science."

Easterlin's reliance on age dynamics and cohort flow seems to have caught the imagination of the press and the public for two reasons. The first is exemplified in the title of the *Psychology Today* article: "The Good News About 1984." Easterlin's demographic predictions fly in the face of Orwellian and journalistic gloom. The second reason for the flurry of attention is that Easterlin's implicit use of the concepts of age dynamics and cohort flow allows an understanding of social, economic and even intellectual trends (such as scholastic performance on standardized tests) solely in terms of the shifting age structure of the population. By analyzing the size of the birth cohort (the group into which a person is born), in relation to the sizes of the older and younger cohorts, fairly accurate predictions can be made about an individual's competitive success in a variety of markets.

Easterlin's analysis is based on age dynamics, or how many people are located at various ages at any given point in time. His claim, which may seem extraordinary, is that age dynamics are at the heart of social and institutional change. Indeed, age dynamics are seen as the driving force behind major social trends and the social successes or failures of individuals. The essential influence on our lives is, according to Easterlin, the shifting relationship between numbers of younger workers and the total population. In simple terms, a scarcity of young workers relative to the population in general (as occurred in the U.S. and Canada in the 1950s) has the effect of reducing competition, so that young workers can enjoy high wages, low unemployment and rapid occupational mobility. This results in higher rates of marriage and higher rates of childbearing. In times of abundant young workers, as during the late 1960s and 1970s, there is increased competition for jobs, lower mobility, limited economic success, reduced rates of marriage and fertility, and higher rates of crime and divorce. For the 1980s, as the supply of workers again declines with the aging of the baby boom generation, Easterlin has predicted a reversal in presently high rates of crime, divorce, unemployment and frustrated mobility. Clearly, economic and social trends, as well as life chances, are contingent on age dynamics and the size of one's birth cohort.

Cohorts are the building blocks of age structure. In a sense, it is the size of cohorts relative to each other that constitutes the essence of age dynamics. Cohort flow is the process of aging from birth to death, by which younger cohorts become adolescent cohorts, which, in turn, are replaced by new cohorts and supersede older cohorts. Cohort flow, in an existential sense, forms the very core of living, aging and dying interspersed with maturation, growth, greater understanding and possibly even wisdom. This process of cohort flow is the means by which a society ages. The youth of one period inevitably matures into the old of another era.

CAUSES OF DEMOGRAPHIC AGING

Since demographic aging, as we have seen, is a process involving relative changes throughout the age structure, it should be clear that its causes are neither simple nor straightforward. In fact, the causes of demographic aging may seem surprising, complex and, at first glance, illogical.

In the recent surge of media concern over our pension system (will it be able to bear the burden of the coming "deluge" of pensioners?) it is easy to forget that an aging population is indicative of prosperity. Countries with the oldest populations are those with the highest standards of living, best nutrition, sanitation and health care and highest levels of industrialization. In other words, an aging population can be seen as a country's measure of success or good fortune.

Factors Contributing to Population Aging

The linking of advanced industrialization and better health care with population aging (a common but incorrectly understood link) has led to the impression that population aging is the direct consequence of increased longevity, or decreased mortality, due to better medical care. However, in Canada, as in most other countries experiencing aging populations, increased life expectancy has contributed only in a minor (and somewhat unexpected) way to population aging. Decreasing mortality tends to have its most pronounced effect on the young, as has been documented throughout the world, not on older members of a population. Declining mortality, in any population, has the seemingly paradoxical effect of making the population somewhat more youthful, rather than more aged. This is because more babies and young children who would otherwise perish now live, thereby lowering the mean age of the population. Many of these young people live to be old enough to reproduce, thereby further adding to the relative youthfulness of the overall population.

Although young people in a population tend to benefit most from declining mortality rates, other age groups benefit as well, though to a lesser degree. In part, this is because adults are less vulnerable to the kinds of diseases, accidents and infectious illnesses to which infants and young children succumb. It is also because the *kinds* of illnesses, accidents and diseases suffered by the adult population, particularly in an advanced industrial nation like Canada, are more resistant to medical or public health intervention. A third reason that adults do not benefit as much from mortality reduction has to do with reaching or approaching the life span ceiling. This means that although enormous strides have been made to enable more of us, in the developed world at least, to live to "a ripe old age," we have still not extended the biological life span very much. Thus a recent Statistics Canada report (1984b, 81), predicts that the very low death rates experienced by Canadians in the past few decades "can be expected to rise in future since the age structure will change as the proportion of elderly people gradually increases." In the most elderly populations in the world, such as in some Western European countries, the death rate has already begun to climb. This is due to the ceiling effect of biological life span, not to deteriorating health status or care.

A more important factor affecting population aging, particularly in Canada, is immigration. Around 1900, Canada welcomed the highest ever recorded number of immigrants. Mostly young people at the time, these immigrants now swell the ranks of the older Canadian population. The importance of immigration is shown by the fact that in 1971 more than one-third of those over 65 were born outside of Canada (Statistics Canada 1976, Table 14). Given that Canada continues to accept immigrants, although at a much lower rate than at the turn of the century, immigration continues to play a role in population aging. The role of immigration now, however, is to contribute to the relative youthfulness of the country and to stave off aging of the population. Given the relative importance of immigration on Canada's fairly small population, changing the levels of immigration, as is being proposed in 1985, could have pronounced effects on projections of Canada's aging population.

The most important contributor to an aging population is declining fertility. At first glance, this may seem surprising and perhaps even incorrect. How is it that Gee (1982, 61) can claim, "population aging is the unplanned byproduct of planned parenthood"? Once explained, however, this is an easy relationship to understand. For our purposes here, let us define a population's age in terms of the proportion of the population that is in the older age groups, say 65 and over. Imagine a hypothetical population in which 25 percent of the population is older (65+), 25 percent younger (under 15) and the remaining 50 percent in the middle age groups (15–64). If the birth rate declines substantially, even for only five years or so, the percentage of the population in the youngest group must decrease in relation to the total, to say 20 percent. This change automatically boosts the proportions constituted by the other two age groups. Once the over 65 group constitutes a greater proportion of the total population than it did earlier, the population is said to be aging. Thus, declining fertility causes the population to age, even if the absolute numbers of older people remain the same.

To look at it another way, let us examine the two population pyramids in Figure 1.1. A population pyramid consists of two bar graphs laid back to back, to provide a conceptual image of how a population's age-sex structure looks. Males and females are on opposite sides. Each bar represents the

FIGURE 1.1
POPULATION PYRAMIDS, CANADA, 1881 AND 1976

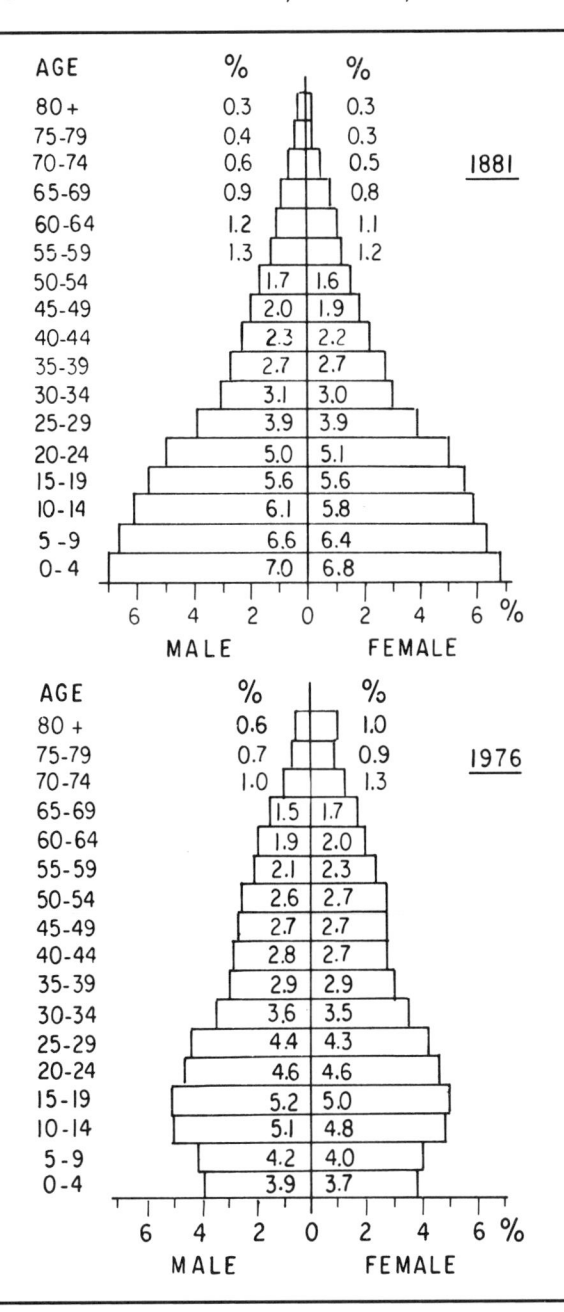

AGE	% (Male)	% (Female)
80+	0.3	0.3
75-79	0.4	0.3
70-74	0.6	0.5
65-69	0.9	0.8
60-64	1.2	1.1
55-59	1.3	1.2
50-54	1.7	1.6
45-49	2.0	1.9
40-44	2.3	2.2
35-39	2.7	2.7
30-34	3.1	3.0
25-29	3.9	3.9
20-24	5.0	5.1
15-19	5.6	5.6
10-14	6.1	5.8
5-9	6.6	6.4
0-4	7.0	6.8

1881

MALE — FEMALE

AGE	% (Male)	% (Female)
80+	0.6	1.0
75-79	0.7	0.9
70-74	1.0	1.3
65-69	1.5	1.7
60-64	1.9	2.0
55-59	2.1	2.3
50-54	2.6	2.7
45-49	2.7	2.7
40-44	2.8	2.7
35-39	2.9	2.9
30-34	3.6	3.5
25-29	4.4	4.3
20-24	4.6	4.6
15-19	5.2	5.0
10-14	5.1	4.8
5-9	4.2	4.0
0-4	3.9	3.7

1976

MALE — FEMALE

SOURCE: For 1881. Dominion Bureau of Statistics. *1921 Census of Canada*, Vol. 2, Table 4. For 1976, Statistics Canada, *1976 Census* Catalogue No. 92-823. Table 11. See also Ellen Gee, "Population." Chapter 10 in Robert Hagedorn (ed.), *Essentials of Sociology*, p. 307 (Toronto: Holt, Rinehart and Winston, 1981).

number of people of each age and sex in the population. The first population pyramid has a wide base, gently sloping sides and a pointed top. The Canadian population of 1881 has experienced high birth rates over a long period of time, and relatively high but consistent death rates, with no major famines, wars or other disasters. Thus a population pyramid may be seen as an imprint of a population's history over the preceding 70-90 years. The 1881 population has a relatively low proportion of its total population in the older age groups. By contrast, the second pyramid (for 1976) is more rectangular in shape. By 1976, Canada has experienced a declining birth rate and low death rates over a long period of time. The proportion of the population over the age of 65 makes up a greater part of the total. This 1976 population is aging; it is relatively older as a direct function of its declining birth rate.

Thus, population aging, although caused by a number of factors, is due in large part to declining fertility. Gee's comment that population aging results from planned parenthood therefore seems apt. Demographic aging could be said to be one unplanned consequence of having smaller families and fewer children in Canadian society. (The fact that Canadians, Americans, Western Europeans, Japanese, and recently the Chinese, have fewer children than people in other countries is itself the result of a complex set of social forces, forces not inseparable from those of population aging.)

The Demographic Transition and Population Aging

The demographic transition, a concept discussed in most introductory sociology texts, has been subjected to sharp criticism as being neither a theory nor an accurate description of historical fact (Beaver 1975). However, it remains a useful way to depict the relationship between mortality decline and fertility decline in a socio-economic context. It must be kept in mind that demographic transition is only a loose depiction, not an actual historical record nor a projection of what Third World countries of today might or should do.

Demographic transition theory cites four major stages in population history. The first is a pre-industrial stage, characterized by high birth rates and high but fluctuating death rates. In this stage, births and deaths are fairly closely balanced, so that population growth is small, and at times nonexistent. The second stage sees a rapid decline in death rates due to control of infectious illnesses and the establishment of stable food production. (In the case of Third World countries, this is due to the importation of sanitation, vaccination and public health measures.) Birth rates, during the second stage, remain largely unchanged and may even increase somewhat due to the improved likelihood of fetuses surviving the gestation period. This stage is characterized by rapid population growth as birth rates outrun death rates. The third stage occurs when birth rates start to decline. In today's industrialized countries, this is due to recognition of the economic and social utility of smaller families. In Third World countries, it is hoped, this decline in birth rates will result from similar recognition, accompanied by economic development and aided by the importation of contraceptive technology. The fourth stage occurs when nations become fully industrialized and birth rates and death rates are low and balanced. At this stage, many countries of the industrialized world are approaching or have reached zero population growth.

Each of these stages corresponds to stages of population aging. A country with very high birth rates and high death rates is a demographically young country with a low median age and a small, often negligible, population in the older ages. People are struggling against famine, war and a very uncertain future, both as individuals and societies. The second stage sees an extension of life expectancy, particularly for young children, as mortality declines, although the burgeoning birth rate tends to keep the population young. At the third stage, when the birth rate begins to decline, populations begin the aging process. Nations at stage four, particularly those at zero population growth, are among the oldest populations in the world.

The results of a computer simulation of an artificial stable population (United Nations 1954) reveal the enormous importance of fertility decline in population aging. Table 1.1 shows the effect on the proportion of the population in the older age groups of comparable declines in fertility and mortality. It is clear that populations age largely in response to declining fertility rates.

MEASURES OF DEMOGRAPHIC AGING

The basic challenge in assessing the degree to which a population is aging is two-fold: to find a measure that accurately reflects the changing age struc-

TABLE 1.1

RELATIVE EFFECTS ON AGING OF MORTALITY AND FERTILITY DECLINES

	Percent Change in Population Aged 60 Years and Over
Effect of mortality decline (increase in life expectancy from 40 to 70)	+0.7%
Effect of fertility decline (reduction from 4.0 to 1.0 in Gross Reproduction Rate)	+18.9%

SOURCE: United Nations, "The Cause of the Aging of Populations: Declining Mortality or Declining Fertility," *Population Bulletin of the United Nations* 4:34 (New York: United Nations, 1954).

ture of a population, and to develop guideposts for determining when a particular population is aged. Of course, the latter challenge is less of a problem when a single population is assessed over time; in this case, whether the population is considered aged, according to international criteria, matters less than the fact that changes in age composition are discernible over time. It is when comparisons are made *among countries* that the question of whether or not a given population is aged becomes important.

Finding a measure that reflects changes in age structure depends, in large degree, on how demographic aging is defined. For example, if aging is defined as growth in the older population relative to that below a certain age, say 65, then the measure of aging might simply be the percentage of the population that is 65 years and older at any given time. If the definition of aging is relational, then the measure might be one of economic dependency of older persons on those in the labour force. Still other measures attempt to capture overall changes in the age structure of a population. In the section below, several standard approaches to measurement, along with some newly conceived, innovative approaches, are discussed, critiqued and compared with an eye toward relating measurement and conceptualization of the aging process.

Proportion of Elderly People in the Population

The most frequently used index of population aging is the percentage of older people in the population. (Selecting 65 as the age at which one is considered old is clearly a social convention. In societies where the average life expectancy is 50 years, the entry point into old age would obviously not be 65. Similarly, in advanced agricultural societies in which retirement is virtually unknown, the point at which one is considered to be an elder of the community is less clearly specified.) Measuring population aging in terms of the proportion of the population over the age of 65 (or some other arbitrary age) is intended as a reflection of the process of aging in a population. As the percentage of the elderly grows, the population is said to age. It is a simple measure, and one that seems, at least on first glance, to reflect demographic aging in a single, easily understood index.

One of the problems with this measure is that it may create the idea that demographic aging involves only two dichotomous groups. Variations occurring among other groups in the population, for example, the very young or those of labour force age, are overlooked. The result could be a false impression of the seriousness of the problem potentially created by the population aging. For example, two different populations could have the same proportion over 65, say 17 percent. In the one that had had a constant rate of reproduction over the past half century or so, the percentage of people aged 14 would be around 23, and the percentage of those in the labour force would be around 60. The other population, with exactly the same proportion in the elderly group, would have a youthful component comprising 15 percent of the total and a labour force age group comprising 68 (Friedlander and Klinov-Malul 1980, 53). Clearly, these two populations are experiencing very different demographic and economic situations. To treat them as identical with respect to demographic aging would be a serious error.

As stated earlier, it has long been established that the process of demographic aging is, to a large degree, a direct consequence of declining fertility in situations of low mortality (Coale 1956; Hermalin 1966, United Nations 1954). The populations of both Canada and the United States have been aging consistently since 1900, according to the index that measures the proportion of the population 65 years and older. If population aging is a function of declining fertility, then one might conclude that fertility in these two countries has been consistently declining. This is not the case; fertility rates rose fairly dramatically in the 1940s and 1950s in both countries. This shift is age structure is not reflected at all by the simple index of aging (Kii 1982, 440-441).

The age group over 65 has been subdivided into further categories (Neugarten 1974), in an attempt to better reflect the changing age structure within the older population. These subcategories are variously defined but generally known as: the young-old (65-74), the middle-old (75-84), the old-old (85-90) and the frail-old (90 plus). Although subject to some of the same problems as the basic index, these subdivided indices enable us to see that in Canada, for example, the oldest age group, aged 85 and over, is growing faster than the younger two groups of elderly (Health and Welfare Canada 1983, 18). This has clear and obvious implications for planning health care resources and other facilities and services.

Dependency Ratios and Old/Young Ratios

Another ratio sometimes used as an index is the ratio of those over 65 to those of labour force age. This is generally known as the *old age dependency ratio*. The assumption here is that older groups in the population are for the most part retired from the labour force and therefore dependent economically on those who are working, for pensions and other forms of support. (There is also a youth dependency ratio, made up roughly of those aged 0-17 in relation to those 18-64, but this is not of concern here.)

Given the roughness of this index, it fails to account for high unemployment or other forms of dependency among segments of the work force, or for members of the elderly who continue to work and are not dependent in any way. Thus, the crude assumption of dependence does not tap the economic realities of either the older population or those who are working, and can distort the degree of "burden" felt at any given time. Although useful as a gross indicator, and free of some of the biases of the index using simple percentage of elderly, the old age dependency ratio is not a sensitive index of aging nor an accurate reflection of possible economic problems caused by an aging population.

Instead of a dependency ratio, other ratios of the older population to younger populations have been used as measures of demographic aging. Among these are the ratio of those aged 65 and over to young people aged 15-19 or 16-25. In times of stiff competition for scarce jobs, these two groups of people may be similarly vulnerable to job loss or to difficulties in finding a job after being laid off (McPherson 1983, 77). The degree of competition between them, purely in terms of their numbers, may reveal to some degree the relationship between shifting age structure and economic opportunities. This too, however, is an artificial index of population aging. Like proportion of people over 65, it dichotomizes the population. Both measures overlook shifts that occur in other age groups. The 65 plus young people ratio is even more selective in this regard than is the proportion 65 and over.

A third ratio used to measure aging in populations is the ratio of those over 65 to those under 15 years. This is considered a basic and fairly accurate measure of demographic aging, since its conceptual basis is the relation between those most affected by aging and those most affected by rejuvenation resulting from fertility (Rossett 1964). The question as to whether or not a population is aging, when there is an increase in both the proportion over 65 and that under 15, can be answered fairly readily by this index. For example, let us suppose that a population has 25,000 persons (25 percent of the total) under the age of 15, and 12,000 over 65. The young/old index would be .48. If the older and the younger group each gain 5,000 additional members over a given period of years, the old/young index becomes .56, indicating that this hypothetical population is, in fact, aging. Note that this occurs in spite of equal numbers of new entrants to both the young and the older age groups.

Despite its sensitivity to the dynamics of demographic aging, the old/young index is not without problems. A central concern is that the bulk of the population in most low-mortality countries, those aged 16-64, is excluded from the index. It has also been found that the old/young index tends to be overly sensitive to birth rate changes and tends to exaggerate the degree of population aging when fertility decreases sharply (Kii 1982, 439). This is because the index does not include age structure changes that occur in the large age group in the middle.

Another measure based on age ratio is that devised by Easterlin (1978). Rather than focussing on the very old and the very young, or the ratio of retirement age population to working age population, Easterlin focusses only on those of labour force age — a ratio of younger to older workers. When younger workers are abundant, wages are lower, unemployment higher and mobility prospects dimmer. When youthful workers are scarce, their economic prospects improve. Although this is not a measure of demographic aging in the strict sense, Easterlin's compelling evidence, drawn from a study of wages, mobility, unemployment, crime, educational testing and the women's movement for equal rights, does reveal a clear relation between age structure and economic opportunity. Further, he indicates that future fertility is in part a function of the ratio of younger to older workers. When young workers face stiff competition for jobs, fertility declines. Hence future populations, although probably older in demographic terms, are likely to face better economic prospects. Easterlin's analysis, discussed in more detail later in this chapter and the next, provides evidence of the complexity of the relationship between age structure changes and economic factors.

Median Age

Used as a single index of population aging, the median age is not bound to an arbitrary entry point into old age. The median age is simply an age at the midpoint of a population: 50 percent of the population is older than the median and 50 percent younger. Generally, populations with median ages of 30 or more (Canada's in 1981 was 29.6) are considered old, while those with a median age of 20 or lower are considered young (Shryrock and Siegel 1975).

The median age was dismissed by Rossett in 1964 as an inadequate measure of demographic aging. He cited the case of France, which, when measured by the percentage of the population 65 and over, ranked as the world's most aged country, while it ranked only eleventh when median age was used as the measure of aging. Despite this complaint, Kii (1982, 441) finds that "median age is the best approximation among the conventional indices for measuring the degree and trend of population aging." Median age, however, is found to be particularly sensitive to rapid growth among the youngest groups of society, even when birth rates start to fall off, as they did in Canada in the 1960s. The median age change from 26.3 in 1961 to 29.6 in 1981 (Statistics Canada, 1984c) suggests that the population was not aging much, despite a precipitous decline in the birth rate during this period.

Years Remaining until Death

Given all the problems associated with measures of aging based on years lived since birth, either in terms of ratios or proportions, and the difficulties involved in establishing the point of entry into old age, Ryder (1975) proposed a new measure of aging based on years remaining until death. Rather than arbitrarily designating the point at which a person enters old age, recognizing how variable this is across ethnic and racial groups, sexes and socio-economic groups, Ryder suggests that a person enters old age when he/she has, on average, ten years of life remaining. Although not commonly used, this measure is useful because it allows a floating entry point to old age, different for women and men, for natives and non-natives, for city dwellers and country residents, for workers and for company presidents. It allows differential life expectancy among sub-groups to be built into the measure of aging. For example, among the lowest income group of males in Canada in the late 1970s, old age would begin at 57, while for the highest income males, it would begin at almost 64 (Wilkins and Adams 1983, 1078). For women, the comparable figures for income groups would be 62 and 66. It is notable that even for the highest income males in Canada, old age does not begin at 65 (the conventional age), but a year earlier.

Despite the advantages of Ryder's measure, it is not without weaknesses. Most notably, this measure, like the proportion of the population over age 65, tends to dichotomize the population. In Ryder's measure the two categories are somewhat blurred, but essentially they are: those with ten years or less left to live, and those with more than ten years left to live. As with the simple proportion of those 65 and over, Ryder's measure tends to oversimplify demographic aging. A further problem is that it seems to be insensitive to changes in fertility and age structure. Years remaining, in short, seems to be a more appropriate measure of differential longevity than of population aging. However, it is of particular use in assessing differences among sub-groups as to age of entry to old age (Jackson 1980).

Disability-free Life Expectancy

Like Ryder's measure based on years remaining until death, disability-free life expectancy (Wilkins and Adams 1983) is an attempt to include more than years lived or the percentage of population over and under an arbitrary cutoff point designated as the beginning of old age. Disability-free life expectancy, like Ryder's measure of years remaining until death, is an attempt to differentiate among subgroups on survivorship. In addition, it focusses on quality of life. This measure, developed in Canada, relies on subtraction of the expected years of long-term institutionalization and disability (derived from the Canada Health Survey conducted in 1978-79) from expectation of life. According to this index, a low income man in Canada enters old age at 49, while a high income man enters old age at 60. At this point, each has ten years remaining of disability-free life (Wilkins and Adams 1983, 1078). For women, the entry point to disability-free old age is 60 for the poorest, and 65 for the most well-to-do.

Although subject to the same criticisms as the index of years remaining until death, this sophisticated index allows an examination of how the later years of life differ from one group to another. It permits some degree of insight into the real economic burdens placed on certain subgroups of society. For example, it becomes clear as a result of analysis with this index that "a shorter life expectancy among the poor is not compensated for by less disability" (Wilkins and Adams 1983, 1077). In fact, poor men lose, on average, almost eight years of good life (disability-free) compared to the 4.2 lost by the high income men.

The Slope of the Population Pyramid

The last index of population aging to be discussed here is also newly developed (Kii 1982). It is based on the notion that the aging of a population is not simply growth of the older population, but rather a process of change that occurs throughout the entire age structure of a population. This measure avoids the difficulties of arbitrary categorization or of possible distortions implicit in ratios between various age groups. Essentially, this measure quantifies the slope of the population pyramid, which is a depiction of age structure on a bar graph from 0 to 100, with males and females on opposite sides. It has been clearly shown by demographers that the shape of a population pyramid reflects changes in fertility and mortality over time. A young population has a wide base and gently sloping sides, while an older population tends to be more rectangular than pyramidal, reflecting the swelling of the older and middle groups and the shrinking of the younger groups. Thus, the slope of the population pyramid, computed by a least squares regression line, is an index of population aging. (A least squares regression line is a single line drawn through a scatter plot of data points on a graph that reflects the overall pattern of the data.) How this works is depicted in Figure 1.2, where it can be seen that in an aging Canadian population, the slope of the pyramid becomes gradually steeper.

This index is more sensitive to changes throughout the age structure than any other measure available. It can reflect simultaneously changes in the proportions of young and old, and changes occurring within the large middle group (those of labour force age). This measure has the further advantage of conceptual clarity. In terms of the two challenges of measuring demographic aging that were cited at the outset of this section — to find a measure that accurately reflects changing age structure and to develop guideposts that show when a population is aged — the slope of the population pyramid is ideal. It reflects well, in a simple measure, the degree to which a population is aging overall. The newness of the measure has not permitted the development of clear cut-off points above which a population is considered aged, but it is likely that these will emerge. Unfortunately, comparative world data using this measure are not yet available.

CONCLUSION

In this chapter we have explored the nature and causes of demographic aging and introduced some of the ways in which it is measured. It should be

FIGURE 1.2
LEAST SQUARES LINE APPLIED TO CANADA, 1901, 1951, AND PROJECTED TO 2001

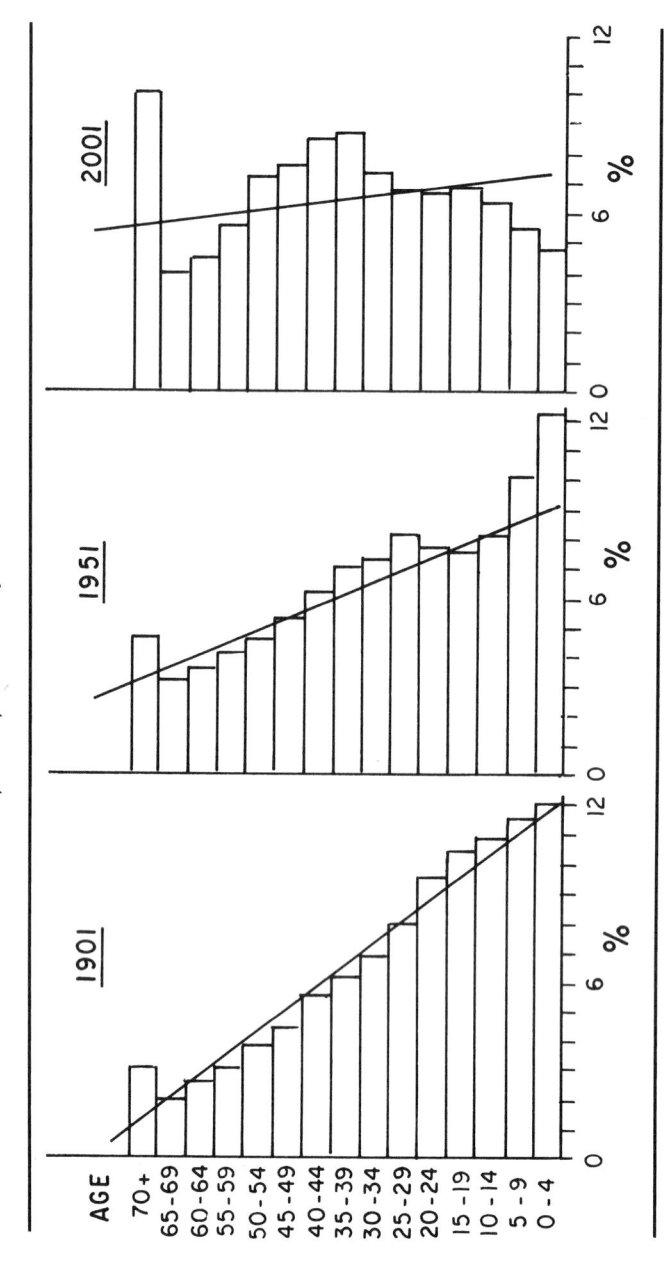

SOURCES: 1901 and 1951 data: Statistics Canada and Social Science Federation of Canada. *Historical Statistics of Canada*, 2nd edition. Edited by F. H. Leacy, Series A78–93, p. A78–93 (Ottawa: Minister of Supply and Services, 1983). 2001 data: Statistics Canada, *Population Projections for Canada, Provinces and Territories 1984–2006* (Catalogue No. 91–520), p. 139 (Ottawa: Minister of Supply and Services, 1985). Projection used here is based on a low-growth scenario: 1.4 children per woman in 1996, net gain of 50,000 a year from international migration.

apparent from this discussion that demographic aging is a complex phenomenon, one that is inextricably bound to the historical and socio-economic circumstances of the country in which it occurs. Further, age structure is dynamic, living, and changing. Fertility changes have profound consequences not only for population aging in the ultimate sense, but for cohort flow and age dynamics, which are a crucial aspect of aging as it occurs throughout the structure of a population.

The next chapter will deal with some of the major approaches taken to analyze the issues involved in population aging. Research approaches will receive the most attention, but theoretical (conceptual) work will also be considered.

CHAPTER 2

PERSPECTIVES ON POPULATION AGING: CONCEPTUAL AND RESEARCH APPROACHES

It is not surprising, given the complexity of the process of demographic aging and its correlation with forces such as economic development, that there is a proliferation of approaches to analysis and explanation. These approaches range from varying conceptualizations of the nature of population aging, to practical policy-oriented analyses of implications. The approaches begin and end at different points and rely on strikingly different assumptions. As might be expected, conclusions drawn from the different approaches range from frank alarmism about population aging to acceptance of aging as a predictable change that requires economic and social adjustments, but not major social upheavals.

Given the recent expansion of the literature on population aging, it would be difficult to comprehensively examine every approach here. The emphasis is on describing and contrasting the main theoretical and research orientations in the field. New developments and recent insights will be highlighted. Specifically, the chapter has three goals. The first is to show how *perspective* influences the approach taken to population aging. Second, the main conceptual and theoretical approaches are discussed and compared. Third, research approaches based on the different theoretical stances are contrasted.

THE POWER OF PERSPECTIVE

The way in which we conceptualize a problem in order to explain or understand it has to do with perspective. To understand the power of perspective, think for a moment about the house in which you grew up, or your grandparents' house perhaps, or any house that means something to you. When you think about this house, you may fondly remember holiday dinners or muse about the time your kitten got stuck under the front porch; you may have some similar emotionally-charged memory. In thinking this way, you are taking a perspective on the house. You are not seeing a total or complete picture of it. It is not that you are necessarily biased (although in this case emotions do tend to alter one's view) but rather that your perspective is so strongly held that you are able to see or recollect events only in one way.

Sometimes a perspective is so strongly held, even without our being aware of it, that changing this perspective involves considerable effort, even pain. To understand this, keep the image of the house to which you feel some attachment firmly in your mind. Now imagine seeing the house through the eyes of a real estate agent. He or she would very likely see things that you might overlook, and might, for example, advise that the room you lovingly painted bright orange when you were fourteen be re-painted to enhance the market value of the house. This suggestion could offend you. It might even be quite difficult for you to abandon your emotional perspective on the house in order to see it from another perspective.

Shifting perspective again, imagine how an artist might see the same house. What you remember as a warm, loving house may appear to the artist's eye as a gothic monstrosity, shaded in greys with long black shadows under the arching eaves. Similarly, a suburban house in which you grew up, as distinctive to you as your own face in a mirror, may appear to the artist as indistinguishable from all other houses in the neighbourhood. This perspective could also be shocking to you. Keep in mind that the house itself has not changed at all. It is still the same shape and size, still made of the same bricks or lumber. The way the house is seen, however, shifts dramatically as perspective is altered.

One last example may serve to illustrate how perspective is often very difficult to change. Keeping your original perspective on the house firmly in mind, imagine the perspective of the demolition expert. This person would certainly not have your fond memories of the house, nor would he/she be concerned about the bright orange bedroom, or the shadows created by the eaves. His/her concern would be solely how to demolish the house most efficiently. He/she would therefore see things in the house that you might never notice, such as the overall support structure. Although the infrastructure is clearly inherent to the house, one perspective provides a clear focus on it, while others tend to overlook this aspect of the house.

The issue of perspective is an important one in studying society, and therefore important in analyzing population aging. Perspective is a lens through which social phenomena are observed, and also a framework by which to analyze social facts or data. For example, it is very difficult to separate the process of demographic aging from the social and economic context in which it occurs (although some demographers try to do this). From one perspective, it is possible to see population aging as the infrastructure of society, the driving force behind other societal changes. From another perspective, population aging can be seen as one of many social variables that interact with other variables in a particular social context. These two perspectives lead to quite different analyses of population aging, as well as different conclusions about the implications of aging. In the first instance, for example, changes in age structure are seen to produce a variety of social changes — in demand for services, in voting patterns, and in family relationships. The conclusion reached from relying on this perspective is probably that population aging is to be viewed with some apprehension. The second perspective, however, sees population aging as occurring simultaneously with economic changes, changing attitudes and changing social policies. The conclusion likely to be drawn from this perspective is that many factors affect and are affected by population aging. This perspective entails less fear and apprehension about the prospects of demographic aging. It tends to be more analytical and detached.

In the social sciences generally, but particularly in sociology, the question of perspective is an important issue of debate; there is considerable confusion around this concept. The social sciences, unlike the natural sciences, lack consensus about the way in which the world ought to be viewed and analyzed. In addition, sociologists regularly argue about the *nature* of perspective. Some see perspective as a part of theory, leading to testable hypotheses that can prove or refute the theory. Others argue that perspective is a way of seeing the social world that no amount of research can show to be correct or incorrect. This latter position recalls the situation described earlier with respect to the house; it would not be possible, or even appropriate, to test whether the perspective of the demolition expert is more correct than that of the person living in the house. To some extent, according to this position, perspective is a product of taste and social circumstance.

Perspective in sociology poses other problems, since sociologists are not only observers and analysts of the social world, but participants in it. This means that the perspective they bring to bear in their sociological research often contains assumptions (or hopes) about what *ought to be*, as well as the standard assumptions about what *is*. This is why the most heated controversies in modern sociology are often arguments about perspective, rather than arguments about methods of research. (Once perspective is in place, the method of analysis generally flows from it.) Like the demolition expert who focusses on the structure of the house and often misses its aesthetic appeal, the sociologist takes a perspective that provides the framework and broad analytical categories for subsequent research. For example, sociologists who see class struggle as a central driving force of social change are likely to use class as a central category in any research that they do.

When studying population aging, the perspective chosen is of central importance, as will be demonstrated in the remainder of this chapter. Perspective determines what is included in the analysis and what is not emphasized. Perspective points up the questions that are important to ask and provides the framework for finding the answers. It sets the stage for research and heads the researcher in the direction of conclusions. Perspective, therefore, is crucially important, not only to research on population aging, but also to the policy implications that often emerge from research.

CENTRAL APPROACHES TO POPULATION AGING

There are two main approaches to the analysis of population aging: the purely descriptive demographic approach, and the structural approach (an attempt to situate population aging in a social and economic context). Within each of these two broad approaches, however, there are many divergences; they are far from monolithic. There is no clear consensus among analysts as to which approach is preferable.

The strictly descriptive analysis is probably the most common approach to population aging in Canada. These descriptive studies are often informative, useful and methodologically sophisticated. Patterns and relationships among demographic forces are graphically revealed. For example, it is by means of these analyses that it becomes clear how changes in fertility affect the process of demographic aging, as was shown in Chapter 1. This type of analysis also enables us, through the use of population projections, to anticipate the future process of population aging.

An alternative approach in analysis of population aging involves focussing on the linkages between demographic phenomena and other social forces, including level of economic development, type of economic system, stratification and other structural variables. This approach is both older and more recent than the descriptive approach. The relationship between demographic structure and social structure was a central concern of early social theorists, such as Thomas Malthus and Karl Marx. However, in the period since World War II (and to some extent prior to that time), this broader approach fell out of favour among mainstream demographers. Social scientists in general had become involved in a quest for acceptance by the more established scientific disciplines. Thus the larger questions were often left behind, in the search for solid and acceptable techniques of data analysis. Recently, however, a number of social scientists have begun to look at the linkages between and among the complex phenomena they observe and analyze. For a growing number of researchers in population aging, the question of the social and economic significance of population aging has emerged as central.

It must be noted that the study of population aging falls not only within the purview of demographers or population analysts. Population aging, particularly when conceptually defined as one of many forces that form the structure of society, is studied by economists, political scientists, gerontologists, policy analysts, health care planners, urban planners, financial analysts, architects, labour leaders and feminists, among others. All these disciplines and groups bring their own special point of view to bear on population aging. The diversity of orientation adds much to our understanding of the nature and dynamics of population aging. However, it makes it difficult in this discussion to decide which approaches to emphasize. Here, only the central features of the basic approaches to population aging will be highlighted.

The Demographic Descriptive Approach

The descriptive approach to population aging examines demographic phenomena apart from the social and economic context in which they occur. The approach has been called *atheoretical*, in that it often lacks a systematic conceptual framework linking population aging with the wider social structure. Analyses of this type regularly make use of the best statistical techniques available for predicting the future pattern of demographic aging. Even when simple and straightforward, these analyses provide other researchers with valuable data to do more theoretically complex studies.

Descriptive demographic analyses enable us to gain an understanding of the process by which populations age. It is possible, for example, to show (as mentioned in Chapter 1) that fertility decline contributes more to population aging than does mortality decline. The way to understand this might be computer simulations in which two hypothetical populations differ only in their rates of fertility. Projecting these two populations over time leads to the conclusion that the population with the more precipitous decline in fertility will age at a faster rate. The emphasis here is on discerning the relationship among demographic factors, and the consequences of relative changes in these factors for population aging. The perspective taken is atheoretical and almost mechanical.

Descriptive studies also add to our understanding of the shifting relationships among groups in the population. For example, the changing ratio of older people to younger people, or to people of working ages, provides a proxy for economic dependency. This can help us envision the changing composition of the population as aging occurs. Although this is a largely technical analysis, the relative impact of the major demographic forces of fertility, mortality and migration (both internal and international) on the various population age groups, and the ratios between them, can be better understood. Such understanding is essential for the detailed planning that must be undertaken to meet the needs of the growing older population relative to the shrinking population of children.

Projecting present trends into the future, a technique of descriptive demographic analysis, is also valuable and necessary. Projections give us a glimpse of what the population will look like some years hence. Typically, the assumptions on which projections are made allow for more than one alternative for each demographic component. For example, the projections prepared by Statistics Canada contain three to five categories of assumptions for each demographic component. The most recent Statistics Canada projections allowed for five categories. The high projection assumes a fertility rate of 2.2 children per woman, a net gain of 100,000 a year from international migration and an internal migration flow that remains constant. By contrast, the low projection assumes a fertility rate of 1.4, a net international gain of 50,000, and the continuation of present trends of internal migration (Statistics Canada 1985, 41). This allows any researcher using the projections to decide on the basis of his/her perspective which set of assumptions are likely to be the correct ones. Projections are generally made from an atheoretical perspective, but they are based on a realistic estimation of what the demographic future holds. Projection studies number among the useful tools provided for researchers and planners by demographers who engage in descriptive analysis.

It could be said that some descriptive analyses seem to have an *implicit* theoretical framework. Descriptive data can be presented in such a way that certain conclusions are almost inevitable. An example of this would be the type of demographic study that reports that the proportion of elderly in the Canadian population is expected to double (or triple or quadruple) within the next x number of years. Without a context in which to situate this information, the public might feel that the future of society is endangered by population aging. With the descriptive approach, then, otherwise atheoretical data analysis becomes a means to convey a certain orientation toward population aging and its consequences. This orientation may or may not emerge from the data analysis itself but provides the framework for the drawing of conclusions and implications about what the data mean.

It has recently been argued, most notably by Myles (1982, 1984) and Phillipson (1982), but also by others, that the time has come to move beyond a descriptive demographic analysis of population aging. These arguments consist of three essential points. The first is that descriptive analysis is not adequate to the task of understanding the complex phenomena involved in population aging. As Myles (1982) eloquently suggests, it is now necessary to move beyond the dependency ratio. The second point made by the critics is that in focussing only on the interaction and interrelationships among demographic phenomena, it is implied that demographic forces are determining other social trends. The danger here is that aging of societies and consequent effects will be seen as the inevitable outcome of demographic dynamics. Hence, there is seen to be a kind of demographic determinism over which we are thought to have little control. The third point is that age structure and socio-economic structure are inextricably bound together. To do simple descriptive analyses of age structure, without clear reference to the circumstances in which changes occur, suggests that demographic reality can be divorced from social life. This, argue critics of descriptive demography, is futile on two counts: 1) it mocks the complexity of social structure, of which age structure forms only a small part, and 2) it gives an unrealistic priority to age structure, which then comes to be seen as the driving force behind all other social change. Given these criticisms, much recent research and conceptual thinking about population aging has moved beyond description and into the realm of structural explanation.

The Structural Approaches

The essential alternative to descriptive demographic analysis of population aging is the structural approach, whereby demographic phenomena are studied not in isolation, but as part of the particular social structural situations in which they exist. There are many structural approaches, only a few of which are discussed here. All share the same basic perspective, in that they all see population aging as embedded in a socio-economic context. The relationships among various demographic phenomena are less interesting, according to this approach, than the relationships between demographic forces and socio-economic structure. The three types of structural approach discussed here are *demographic determinism*, the *crisis approach* and the *contextual approach*.

Demographic Determinism

The demographic determinist view looks for the ways in which age structure determines social structure. At first glance, elements of this approach may appear indistinguishable from the descriptive demographic approach. However, the differences in perspective are profound. In the demographic determinist approach, the relationships among demographic phenomena are not of interest in and of themselves. Rather, it is the consequences of these demographic relationships for society that interest the demographic determinist.

Any number of relationships among demographic phenomena could, potentially, be seen as the driving force behind social change. Most often in reality, however, the important relationships have been the ratio of younger to older workers, or the various dependency ratios. These demographic relationships are then linked to a variety of social and structural changes. In the case of the ratio of younger to older workers, Easterlin (1978) has found that this ratio affects crime rates, rates of divorce and suicide, unemployment, housing demand, fertility and the women's movement, among other social trends. Regarding dependency ratios, many researchers have found that the demand for pensions and for health care rises as the ratio of older to working age populations increases. Others, such as Davis and van den Oever (1981), have suggested that an increase in this ratio increases the likelihood of a "generation gap" between old and young.

Demographic determinism is a compelling explanation of diverse social changes. It allows a simple and straightforward explanation of complex phenomena such as crime rates, which it defines as a direct consequence of the lessened demand for young workers, who, in frustration, turn to crime. Further, it enables a society to attribute responsibility for social problems to shifts in age structure. If policy-makers are convinced that social problems originate in the realm of demography, they can feel, legitimately, little compulsion to act to solve these problems. It is clear that much of the recent research on demographic aging takes a demographic determinist view, either explicitly or implicitly. Usually this is expressed in terms of concern about the increasing ratio of pensioners to the working population, which, it is thought, will reshape our social institutions. Sometimes this perspective approaches that of the crisis perspective, which is discussed next, but often it simply accepts that shifting age structure is the force behind social change.

There are many dangers inherent in the demographic determinist perspective, in addition to the possible justification for inaction by policy-makers. One danger is that age structure may tend to be seen as reflective of social stratification, so that all older people, for example, are seen as economically dependent, while all working-age people are seen as self-supporting. This obvious oversimplification of economic dependency in order to fit prescribed demographic categories masks the economic dependency that exists among some working age people, most notably among women but also among the disabled, the unemployed, and college and university students. It also fosters the notion that all older people are economic burdens, a clearly incorrect idea, but one that can perpetuate stereotypes and lead to prejudice against older people, as well as fear that their presence will cause an economic crisis.

Another danger of the demographic determinist perspective is that it fails to recognize the changes that can occur over time in populations with similar age profiles. For example, older people whose formative years were shaped by the Depression are a rather different group than those whose youth was spent in the relative affluence of the 1950s. These differences in generations are overlooked by demographic determinists, as they lump all people of certain ages together and then assume similarities in lifestyle, health status, economic status and even length of life.

The Crisis Approach

The crisis approach often begins with demographic determinism and moves one step beyond. It is structural in that the central focus is on the effects of demographic forces on social structure. Unlike strict demographic determinism, however, the crisis approach moves into the realm of alarmism; it poses the question as to whether the social structure will be able to change sufficiently to meet the needs of the growing proportion of the population which is and will be older.

In some ways, the present-day crisis approach to population aging resembles the nineteenth century Malthusian view that population growth would outrun food supply, if left unchecked. The contemporary fear is that growth in the older population will outrun the ability of society to provide pensions and health care. Like Malthus, modern-day alarmists ignore analysis of the assumptions underlying their conclusions. Malthus overlooked crucial issues of food distribution and changes in agricultural techniques that would permit greater yields. He also overlooked the cultural, social and economic factors that encourage people to limit their family sizes, even in the absence of modern contraception. Similarly, the present-day crisis perspective on population aging tends to ignore or de-emphasize the capacity of human societies to transform themselves to meet new challenges. To the extent that older people are assumed to be a single homogeneous group requiring pensions and increased amounts of health care, a certain amount of ageism, or prejudice against older people, is present in the crisis perspective as well.

The crisis approach does not take into consideration the degree to which population aging, and the means to deal with any problems it may create, are embedded in the socio-economic structure of societies. For example, population aging is a different problem in an agricultural society than in a modern industrial society (Palmore and Manton 1974; Baker 1983). The status of older people and the esteem in which they are held vary from society to society. This is not merely cultural variability, but a consequence of the kinds of relationships people have to the economic system. Older people in agricultural societies are not redundant to the same degree as in industrial societies. Thus, older people have higher status in agricultural economies than in capitalist industrial economies. This may explain why the crisis approach to aging is so prevalent in capitalist industrial societies, where workers are seen as a burden when they retire.

The Contextual Approach

As stated earlier, there has been a recent resurgence of interest in situating the causes and consequences of population aging within the complex social reality. Population aging cannot be divorced from systems of stratification, economic structure, attitudes toward dependency and productivity, and other social factors. For lack of a better term, we call these various approaches the contextual approach.

Within the contextual approach, there is more than one perspective. Commonly, in Canada today, the contextual approach takes the form of functionalism. That is, each part of society is analyzed for ways in which it is functional for society. Careful research is necessary into the means by which each realm of society is linked to other realms. According to the functionalist perspective, population aging would require society to adapt by changing its institutions, its distribution of wealth and its attitudes to meet the new needs of an aging population. This, however, is not viewed as an insurmountable task, only one that requires reallocation of resources and re-education so that people can better face the new situation. Thus, planning for the future becomes of central importance.

An alternative contextual approach is the neo-Marxist or critical approach, which is growing in popularity in Canada. This approach sees the problem of population aging as lying not in demographic structure, but in the economic system, essentially. For example, Myles (1982), using this approach, concludes that it is not surprising that an aging population is viewed with apprehension in a society premised on economic growth and accumulation of wealth. An aging population is thought, under a capitalist system, to be depleting the storehouses of accumulated wealth. It is also feared to be consuming less in terms of goods, and therefore contributing less to economic growth.

CONCLUSION

In this chapter, various perspectives, or approaches, used to conceptualize and analyze population aging have been examined. The perspective chosen is crucial in determining what is analyzed, how it is analyzed, and what conclusions are drawn. The descriptive demographic approach has been contrasted with the major structural approaches to demographic aging. The demographic descriptive approach analyzes demographic phenomena in isolation from social context. The structuralists see aging as embedded in the structure of society and therefore inseparable from that society. The three structural approaches discussed here are demographic determinism, the crisis approach and the contextual approach. Each has merits, of course, as well as drawbacks. Throughout this book, various approaches are drawn on to analyse Canada's aging population. The most commonly used approach in this book, however, is the structural, contextual one.

CHAPTER 3

DEMOGRAPHIC AGING: THE CANADIAN EXPERIENCE IN WORLD CONTEXT

In discussing Canada's place in world patterns of demographic aging, consideration is given to past trends, present realities and future prospects. The picture that emerges is rather like that produced by a kaleidoscope. The tendencies remain the same but the overall picture shifts. Perspective is shown to play a large role in how Canada's demographic aging situation is perceived. For example, in comparison to the world's demographically oldest countries, Canada is rather youthful. Yet in comparison to what Canada was at the turn of the twentieth century, it has become vastly older. Similarly, in world context, today's less developed countries are beginning to age. In comparison to developed countries, however, they are still youthful indeed.

DEMOGRAPHIC AGING IN WORLD CONTEXT

Demographic aging is occurring to varying degrees all over the world. This trend, begun in many countries in the early part of the twentieth century, is expected to continue into the next century. Siegel (1981) notes that in 1975, 5.3 percent of the world's population was 65 years and older. By 1980 (United Nations 1984), the figure had climbed to 6 percent. It is predicted that by the turn of the century, the proportion of the world's population over 65 years old will well exceed 6 percent (Health and Welfare Canada 1983, 12).

Of course, not all parts of the world are equally old in demographic terms. It is the most economically developed countries that have the oldest populations. In 1980, for example, the developed world had 11.1 percent of its population over age 65, while the developing or third world had only 4 percent over 65 (Health and Welfare Canada 1983, 13). By 2000, Siegel (1981) predicts, these percentages will rise to 12.6 and 4.4 respectively.

Rather than risk boring readers with table after table on world population patterns, we have selected tables that illustrate salient points.

Sex and Age Groups in World Aging

Although it is widely recognized that demographic aging, as a phenomenon, is more advanced in developed than in developing parts of the world, it might be argued that this view contains elements of cultural bias. As mentioned in Chapter 1, there is nothing sacred about the designation of age 65 as the entry point to old age; this is a social convention established in western countries. When we use this arbitrary age in world context to determine the relative age of countries, we could be said to be applying an inappropriate, culturally determined measure. For example, it might be that populations in Africa, Asia or Latin America are actually older, in demographic terms, than we have acknowledged. If a country's people has a life expectancy of 50, for example, and 20 percent of the population is between 40 and 50 years old, then this country might be considered old, even though it may have few people over the age of 65. Nonetheless, most world statistics on aging rely on this conventional, Western measure.

It is clear from Table 3.1, which compares major regions of the world by population over the age of 65, that the most economically developed parts of the world are the most elderly. North America, however, is not the demographically oldest region. First place falls to Europe. Second is North America, with the U.S.S.R. running a close third. As might be expected, those regions ranking among the youngest, by this measure, are Latin America, Asia and Africa. These regions contain the least economically developed countries in the world, some of which have barely begun the demographic transition. However, all three regions also contain countries with relatively advanced economies and relatively high life expectancies. Examples might include Hong Kong and Singapore in Asia, Egypt and South Africa in Africa, and Argentina in South America.

TABLE 3.1
PERCENTAGES OF POPULATION AGED 65 AND OVER, BY SEX, FOR MAJOR REGIONS OF THE WORLD, 1980

	Total	Male	Female
World	6	5	7
Africa	3	3	3
America	7	6	8
North America	11	9	12
Latin America	4	4	5
Asia	4	4	5
Europe	13	11	15
Oceania	8	7	9
U.S.S.R.	10	6	13

SOURCE: United Nations, *Demographic Yearbook, 1982*, Table 2, pp. 132-33 (New York: United Nations, 1984). Copyright, United Nations (1984). Reproduced by permission.

Table 3.1 further reveals that demographic aging favours women. In all regions except Africa there is a greater proportion of women than men in the age group above 65. The gap between the sexes is the largest in the most demographically aged regions. The widest gap of all occurs in the U.S.S.R., a difference accounted for by the enormous losses of men during the Second World War (including those who would have been 65 and over in 1980). The preponderance of women in older populations is due to women's longer life expectancy. The reasons for this longer expectancy are not entirely clear and are still being studied, but some aspects are known. Women have benefitted more than men from public health and medical advances in the past half century. They have also been exposed less, and have exposed themselves less, to environmental risks such as industrial accidents, workplace pollution, and smoking and drinking to excess. However, evidence from controlled studies of monks and nuns, who have almost identical lifestyles and do similar work, suggests that there may be a biological advantage, as well, to being female (Madigan 1968). If this is so, the long-accepted idea that women are the weaker sex may have to be re-evaluated.

The fact that aging populations throughout the world are composed disproportionately of women has multiple social implications. First, there are economic concerns, particularly since relatively few women who are now in the older age groups worked outside their homes during their younger years. In many countries, including Canada, this means that they are eligible for only limited pensions in old age, if indeed they can collect any pensions at all. This is why alarm bells are sounded (by some) about the economic burden of an aging population. (Chapter 4 will provide further discussion of the problem.) A second issue is that older women, in Western society at least, tend to have very low social status. The image of future populations comprised of what are derisively termed "little old ladies" may be unwelcome to many people. Thus the stance taken by the popular press, as well as by some researchers, that an aging population is to be feared, worried about, and avoided if possible.

Table 3.2 avoids some of the problems associated with assessing the degree of population aging on the basis of a single measure by comparing three major age groups. This table contains data for the most demographically aged countries in the world, and presents the most recently available data. Most of these countries are in Europe, as might have been predicted from Table 3.1. Canada stands out among these countries on two counts. First, it is the only country among the most demographically aged countries with less than 10 percent of its population 65 and over. Second, Canada is the only country on the list with more than 20 percent of the population in the age group 0-14. For both these reasons, Canada is, relatively speaking, the least old of the oldest populations in the world. It should be noted further that Canada could be in a favourable economic position, in having the highest proportion of its population in the labour force age range.

The countries that have the highest proportion of their populations over

TABLE 3.2
PERCENTAGE DISTRIBUTION OF THE POPULATION, BY THREE AGE GROUPS, FOR SELECTED INDUSTRIALIZED COUNTRIES, EARLY 1980S

	Age Groups		
	0-14	15-64	65+
Belgium (1979)	19.0	65.4	14.3
Canada (1981)	22.5	67.8	9.7
Federal Republic of Germany (W. Germany) (1981)	16.5	67.2	15.3
France (1982)	20.5	64.5	13.5
Hungary (1981)	20.7	64.8	13.1
Norway (1981)	20.5	63.3	14.9
Sweden (1981)	18.1	64.3	16.5
Switzerland (1982)	17.8	67.2	13.9
United Kingdom (England and Wales (1981)	19.0	64.4	15.2
United States (1981)	20.8	66.3	11.4

SOURCES: Statistics Canada, *1981 Census of Canada* (Ottawa). All other data: United Nations, *Demographic Yearbook, 1982*, Table 7, pp. 178-240 (New York: United Nations, 1984). Copyright, United Nations (1982). Reproduced by permission.

the age of 65 are Sweden, the United Kingdom and West Germany. All three have low proportions in the youngest age group. There are other countries with low proportions of young people, such as the United States, but they do not have comparable older populations. All the countries listed have favourable proportions of their populations in working age groups, with Canada in the best position, followed closely by Switzerland and the United States.

On the basis of this table, several conclusions can be drawn. In the early 1980s, there are many countries older than Canada in demographic terms. None has experienced the dire consequences, economic or social, that have been predicted for the United States and Canada as their populations age. Most of the countries experiencing demographic aging continue to have the majority of their people in the working age groups. Growth in the proportion of the population in the older ages is related to relative shrinkage of the youthful age groups. Lastly, but very importantly, there is little demographic basis for the recent economic difficulties faced by many countries in the Western world. Those countries that are most aged, in population terms, have experienced no more serious recessions or national debt loads than those that are less aged. We may conclude, then, that continued demographic aging, if properly anticipated and planned for, will not necessarily have profound and dire economic consequences.

TABLE 3.3
OLD-AGE DEPENDENCY RATIOS* FOR SELECTED COUNTRIES, 1950–1980, AND PROJECTED TO 2025

	1950	1960	1970	1980	1990	2000	2010	2020	2025
World	9.2	9.5	9.6	9.9	9.8	10.5	10.9	12.7	14.1
More Developed Regions									
Total	11.8	13.5	15.2	17.2	17.5	19.8	20.9	24.3	26.5
Canada	12.2	12.7	12.7	13.1	14.5	15.1	16.5	22.8	27.3
United States	12.5	15.5	15.9	16.2	17.6	16.9	17.0	21.9	25.0
Hungary	10.9	13.8	17.0	20.8	20.7	22.8	24.2	29.2	30.3
Norway	14.7	17.6	20.6	23.2	24.5	22.1	21.5	27.2	29.4
Sweden	15.5	18.1	20.9	25.2	26.6	24.9	27.5	32.9	33.6
U.K.	16.0	17.9	20.6	23.1	23.2	23.1	23.3	27.1	29.2
Belgium	16.2	18.5	21.2	21.8	21.1	23.8	23.5	28.3	31.2
France	17.3	18.8	20.7	21.4	19.7	22.0	21.4	27.0	29.5
W. Germany	14.0	16.0	20.7	22.7	20.1	22.8	28.5	30.0	32.0
Switzerland	14.4	15.2	17.4	20.2	20.8	23.5	28.3	34.0	35.8
Less Developed Regions									
Total	7.8	7.4	7.0	7.0	7.5	7.9	8.5	10.3	11.8

* Ratio of those aged 65 and over to those of labour force age, 15–64.

NOTE: The projections used here, developed by the United Nations, are based on the component method of projection, which considers levels of trends in fertility, mortality and migration separately. Assumptions of the future course of the three components are done country by country and bar the advent of any major catastrophe such as war or famine. The projections in this table rely on medium levels of each of the three components.

SOURCE: United Nations, *Demographic Indicators of Countries: Estimates and Projections as Assessed in 1980*, pp. 58–411 (New York: United Nations, 1982). Copyright, United Nations (1982). Reproduced by permission.

Table 3.3 presents old-age dependency ratios (ratios of those aged 65 and over to those of labour-force age) for the developed and less developed regions of the world, and for the most demographically aged countries, from 1950 and projected to the year 2025. Old-age dependency ratios, although not without problems (as was shown in Chapter 1), attempt to relate the older population to that of labour force age, with the intention of loosely indicating some notion of economic dependency.

Several interesting points are demonstrated in Table 3.3. One is the contrast in the overall trends in old-age dependency ratios between the developed and the less developed regions of the world up until 1980. In the developed world, as in the world as a whole, but in a less pronounced way, the old-age dependency ratio increased consistently and rather strongly from 1950 to 1980. In the less-developed world, in contrast, the old-age dependency ratio declined from 1950 to 1970, and then remained at 7.0 until 1980. After this point, the projections show that both regions of the world will have increasing old-age dependency ratios. However, the rate of increase predicted is considerably steeper for the developed world. In 1950, the difference in the old-age dependency ratio between developed and developing regions of the world was 4 percent. By 2025, the projected difference will be 14.7 percent, a 3.5-fold increase.

A difference this large in population structure between regions that are already worlds apart in terms of standard of living, lifestyle, and degree and nature of economic and social problems, cannot help but add to communication difficulties between the developed and developing countries. Even though both regions of the world may be aging, in terms of having an increasing proportion of their populations above 65 in relation to that of labour force age, the dramatic difference in *degree* of aging is crucial. A society in which the old-age dependency ratio is 26.5, as is predicted for the developed world by 2025, is a profoundly different society than that in which the ratio is 11.8 (predicted for the developing world in the same year). In terms of age structure, the developing countries in the year 2025 would closely resemble those of the developed world of 1950. The potential human energy levels of the populations of the developing world contrast sharply with those of the developed world in the future. These differences may have implications for international politics, as well as for the economics of world trade and balance of power. For example, the developing countries might be able to increase their productivity and increasingly become a source of labour for the developed countries, which would become even more consumption-oriented.

Returning to Table 3.3, we note that every country listed is predicted to age considerably by the year 2025. With the exception of the United States, the old-age dependency ratio by 2025 for every country on the list is predicted to be higher than the average for developed regions as a whole.

This indicates that even in the developed world, these countries are exceptional. Five countries, Hungary, Sweden, Belgium, West Germany and Switzerland, will have old-age dependency ratios above 30, and many other European countries are very close behind. The United States, by comparison, even by 2025, will not have an old-age dependency ratio above that of Sweden in 1980. Canada's ratio by 2025 is predicted to slightly exceed that of the United States and would correspond to the ratio predicted for Sweden in 2010.

The patterns over time in old-age dependency ratios among these oldest countries are worth noticing. The country that experiences the most dramatic increase in old-age dependency ratio by 2025 is Switzerland, which is also projected to have the highest ratio in 2025. France, however, which is predicted to experience a far less dramatic increase in old-age dependency, is close to the top countries by 2025 in terms of old-age dependency ratio. The United States, which is predicted to experience a rate of change comparable to that of France, i.e., a 1 to 3 point increase per decade, ranks the lowest among these countries by 2025 in old-age dependency. Canada, close to the mean ratio for all developed nations, is predicted to experience a greater increase than the United States in old-age dependency. Canada's pattern of increase in this ratio most closely resembles that of Norway or Belgium, which are experiencing moderate rates of population aging.

DEMOGRAPHIC AGING IN CANADA: PAST AND PRESENT

Whether or not Canada is considered to be demographically old depends both on the perspective used to interpret Canadian data, and on the country or world region used as the comparison. Clearly, relative to Sweden, West Germany or the United Kingdom, Canada is youthful. However, in comparison to most countries in Africa or Latin America, Canada is old. If we consider that, in 1981, one out of every ten Canadians was above the age of 65, this could be reason for alarm or not, depending on how we interpret this datum. If population aging is seen as a gradual, inexorable process resulting from declining fertility and shifts occurring throughout the age structure, then continued aging will likely be viewed as requiring an adjustment of priorities and a reassignment of monies. If, however, the continuing process of demographic aging is seen as frightening and not capable of being accommodated economically, then policy changes might be made in an attempt to circumvent the process.

Whatever perspective is taken, by all available measures, there is little doubt that Canada's population is aging. In fact, we have been aging, in the demographic sense, since before the twentieth century began. The reasons for this phenomenon are complex and often misunderstood, but include changing patterns of fertility, immigration and mortality.

Aging in Canada's Past

There is nothing new about Canada's aging population. The number of people over the age of 65 has grown consistently since before the beginning of this century. By 1981, this group numbered 2.4 million, and constituted 9.7 percent of Canada's total population (Health and Welfare Canada 1983, 14). This represents a tenfold increase since 1901, when the population 65 and over, totalling less than 250,000, made up only 5 percent of the total population (Foot 1982, 9). The total Canadian population during this 80-year period increased fourfold.

Table 3.4 shows three indicators of demographic aging for Canada since the time of the first census in 1851. For median age, the most commonly used index of aging, it is clear that the trend in Canada has been a steady increase from the late teens in the latter part of the nineteenth century to close to 30 years by 1981. The median age index, like the percentage of the population 65 and over, reveals two periods — the 1930s and the 1970s — in which Canada's population experienced accelerated aging. Although Canada's median age reached a historically high level in 1981, Foot (1982, 124) calculates that over the next 70 years (until 2051), the population will age as much as it did over the previous 130 years. Further, Foot (1982, 258)

TABLE 3.4
THREE MEASURES OF DEMOGRAPHIC AGING FOR CANADA, 1851 TO 1981

	Median Age	% 65+	Total Dependency Ratio
1851	17.2	2.7	.909
1861	18.2	3.0	.834
1871	18.8	3.7	.828
1881	20.1	4.1	.749
1891	21.4	4.6	.692
1901	22.7	5.0	.651
1911	23.8	4.7	.603
1921	24.0	4.8	.644
1931	24.8	5.6	.592
1941	27.1	6.7	.526
1951	27.7	7.8	.615
1961	26.3	7.6	.712
1971	26.3	8.1	.604
1981	29.5	9.7	.475

SOURCE: David K. Foot. *Canada's Population Outlook: Demographic Futures and Economic Challenges*, p. 9; total dependency ratio data from p. 129 (Toronto: James Lorimer, 1982).

predicts that by 2051, the median age of Canada's population will be around 42 years.

Although Canada's population aging has clearly been continuous, it has not been consistent. Particular attention must be given to the two decades during which Canada's aging process accelerated. The 1931–41 period saw a sizeable jump in both the median age and the percentage of the population 65 years and older. The 1930s, as most people know, were the years of the Great Depression, an unusual historical period. Due largely to poor economic prospects, both birth rates and immigration dropped. The result was a rapid acceleration in population aging. Conversely, during the 1951–61 decade, a period marked by a "baby boom" and high immigration to Canada, both indices of aging reveal that Canada was relatively younger. The largest ten-year increase in aging in Canada occurred during 1971–81, however. This recent period is one of very low birth rates (the lowest in Canada's history), and relatively low levels of immigration. These factors may explain why aging is being viewed now with such concern.

The essential reason for the general trend in aging of Canada's population since 1851 has been a declining birth rate, interrupted periodically by temporary increases in births. Many people have the impression that declining birth rates, like demographic aging, are a recent phenomenon. However, fertility rates have been dropping throughout most of the twentieth century, reaching a low point during the Depression years, but an even lower point in the 1970s and early 1980s (Gee 1981, 291; Grindstaff, 1975). A large but temporary increase in birth rates occurred following World War II, resulting in the baby boom generation.

Accompanying the overall decline in birth rates over the past century has been a general, but far from smooth, decline in the number of new immigrants coming to Canada. This also has contributed to population aging, but to a lesser degree. Immigration, like fertility, is highly responsive to economic conditions. For this reason, immigrants tend to come to Canada in waves. They also leave in waves, emigrating largely to the United States. Early in Canada's history, immigration was the principal contributor to population growth. The largest period of immigration, however, occurred during the first decade of this century, when immigrants came to open up Canada's West. These immigrants, being young, contributed to a rejuvenation of Canada's population. Later, this large group of immigrants added to Canada's older population. It should be reiterated that immigrants tend to rejuvenate a population, as well as contribute economically and socially to society. Declines in immigration rates therefore have the consequence of contributing to population aging.

Table 3.4 also shows the trend in total dependency ratio. This is the ratio of non-working age people (0–14 years and 65 years and over) to people of working age. Intended as a rough indicator of economic dependency, this ratio is a single indicator of age composition change not revealed by the other two measures. It can therefore be useful in formulating policy changes. The reason for using the total dependency ratio rather than the old-age dependency ratio is that the total dependency permits a more realistic glimpse of relative losses of young people, compared to gains of older people. To rely on the old-age dependency ratio could exaggerate the degree of economic burden likely to be felt in future, because gains accrued from a declining birth rate are excluded from this ratio. It has been demonstrated clearly, as shown in Figure 3.1, that a decline in the percentage of children has exceeded growth in the percentage of the elderly. In the year 2021, in Canada, projections indicate that the percentages of children and elderly persons will be equal. Thereafter, it is predicted that the elderly will comprise a greater percentage of the total population than will children.

From the total dependency ratios shown in Table 3.4, it is apparent that the overall trend has been a decline in Canada since 1851. A particularly pronounced decline occurred from 1851 until 1911, followed by a slight in-

FIGURE 3.1

HISTORICAL AND FUTURE AGE COMPOSITION, CANADA, 1851 TO 2051

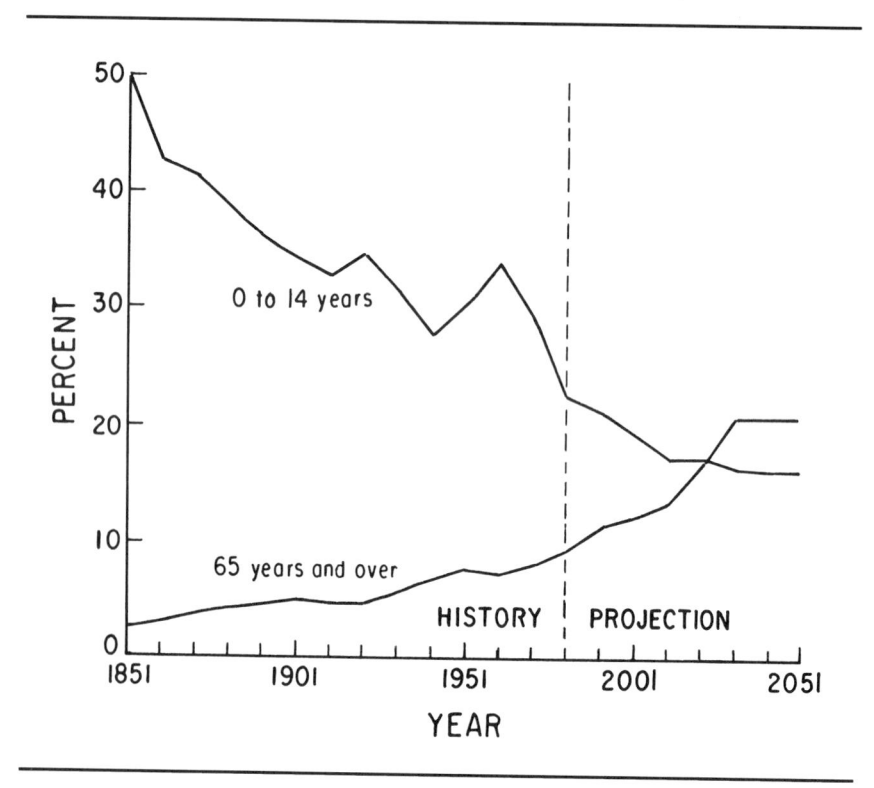

SOURCE: David K. Foot. *Canada's Population Outlook: Demographic Futures and Economic Challenges*, p. 127 (Toronto: James Lorimer, 1982).

crease in 1921. Larger, but still temporary, increases occurred in the 1951 and 1961 decades as a result of the baby boom. The period from 1961 to 1981 saw another precipitous decline. The total dependency ratio is strikingly responsive to changes in the birth rate. In future, however, as the percentages of children and elderly persons become equal, and then as the percentage of the elderly begins to dominate the total dependency ratio, this will not be the case.

As was emphasized in Chapter 1, population aging involves shifts throughout the age structure. Another way to examine the concept of dependency is to analyze trends in the labour force age population. These are shown in Table 3.5. The overall trend is that an increasing proportion of the total population is of labour force age. Temporary declines occurred in the 1921 and 1951-61 decades. These again correspond to increases in birth rates. At no time has the labour force age population made up less than 50 percent of the total. In 1981, two-thirds of the Canadian population was of working age, 7.2 percent more than at the turn of the century. It would seem that Canada's demographic structure is now more able to handle a growing older population, by having an increasing proportion of its population of labour force age and a decreasing proportion of youthful dependents.

Further evidence of Canada's favourable economic position, with respect to age structure, is found in the trends of young versus older working age population, also shown in Table 3.5. There has been a fairly strong increase in the working age population above age 25 since 1851. As with total labour force age population, a sizeable jump occurred between 1971 and 1981, bringing the prime working age population to almost one-half of Canada's total population. This has been accomplished with a negligible decline in the younger (15-24 years) working age population. This means, demographically speaking at least, that proportions of new workers have not declined, while the prime wage earning age population has increased dramatically. Since older workers tend to earn more, on average, than younger workers do, this is an advantageous demographic situation for supporting a growing older group, if necessary.

It should be apparent from this brief historical review of Canadian trends in demographic aging that, although some concern about aging population in Canada is warranted, much of the recent media alarm is not well grounded in fact. Canada's population has been aging gradually for well over a century. The recent media attention to the "problem" of population aging may be partly explained by the acceleration of the process during the 1970s. This trend, of course, is attributable largely to the sharp decline in fertility during this decade. The age structure in Canada at present is such that the bulk of the population is of labour force age, and the proportion of children, although declining, still exceeds the proportion of elderly. It will be some time in the future (approximately 2031) before this relatively favourable demographic situation shifts drastically.

TABLE 3.5
LABOUR FORCE AGE COMPOSITION IN CANADA, 1851 TO 1981

	15-24 years	25-64 years	Total Labour Force Age Population
1851	20.5	31.9	52.4
1861	21.0	33.5	54.5
1871	20.5	34.2	54.7
1881	21.2	35.9	57.1
1891	20.7	38.4	59.1
1901	20.0	40.6	60.6
1911	19.4	43.0	62.4
1921	17.3	43.5	60.8
1931	18.8	44.0	62.8
1941	18.7	46.8	65.5
1951	15.3	46.6	61.9
1961	14.3	44.1	58.4
1971	18.6	43.8	62.4
1981	19.3	48.5	67.8

SOURCE: David H. Foot, *Canada's Population Outlook: Demographic Futures and Economic Challenges*, p. 9 (Toronto: James Lorimer, 1982).

Contemporary Aging Patterns in Canada

It is not the intention of this book to describe dimensions of the older population in Canada. These will be addressed in more detail by subsequent monographs in the Aging Series. However, some contemporary trends and differentials in demographic aging are worthy of particular mention here. Patterns such as the sex difference in aging, aging among the older population, and some subgroup differences in aging are crucial to understanding that demographic aging is not a uniform process. No attempt is made here, however, to comprehensively review contemporary Canadian aging trends and patterns.

Sex Ratio

A striking aspect of the process of demographic aging, as noted earlier in this chapter, is the widening imbalance in the sex ratio. In Table 3.1, it was noticed that there is a greater preponderance of women among the demographically oldest populations in the world. The sex imbalance that accompanies demographic aging is an important policy concern both now and for the future, for largely economic, but also social reasons. Women more often than men tend to be financially dependent. When women work outside the home they earn, on average, 60 to 70 percent of what men earn. They also have full pension plans available to them less often. When they do not work outside the home, they are dependent on their husbands' pension plans to provide for their old age. Often these are inadequate or simply cease payment (or decrease payment considerably) on the death of the principal wage earner (Dulude 1984). Since Canadian women in the past worked outside the home less often than they do now, their financial plight in their older years is often considerable. Given the longer life expectancy of women, the dependency burden on society and the poverty faced by older women create a serious societal challenge. Some of the concerns raised for women by demographic aging will be discussed in more detail in Chapter 4, with attention to policy implications in Chapter 5.

As Canada's population continues to age, the sex imbalance is predicted to worsen. Until the mid-1950s, men in the 65 and over group slightly outnumbered women (Health and Welfare Canada 1983, 21). By the 1960s, women had come to predominate. By 1981, the ratio of females to every 100 males had become 124 for the age group 65-79 and 184 for the age group 80 and above (Health and Welfare Canada 1983, 2). The numerical predominance of older women is greater in the large metropolitan areas. In rural areas, older men outnumber older women. Over half the women aged 70 and over in 1981 in Canada were widows (Health and Welfare Canada 1982, 2). By the year 2051, it is projected that the sex ratio will be 134 females per 100 males aged 65-79, and 218 females for every 100 males in the 80 plus age group (Health and Welfare Canada 1983, 21).

Place of Residence

Of the total population aged 65 and over in Canada, the largest percentage, almost 37 percent, lives in Ontario (Health and Welfare Canada 1982, 1), with high numbers as well in Quebec and British Columbia. The provinces with the highest proportions of their populations in the older groups are Prince Edward Island, Saskatchewan and Manitoba (Health and Welfare Canada 1983, 24). Prince Edward Island is the province with the highest proportion of its population over 80 years old (3 percent in 1981 compared to 1.9 percent for all Canada).

The majority of Canada's older people live in urban areas, with 40 percent living in centres of one-half million or more (Health and Welfare Canada 1983, 26). Rural areas, contrary to popular myth, had only one in 20 people over the age of 65 in 1981 (Health and Welfare Canada 1982, 26). However, there are a number of small towns, notably in Manitoba and Saskatchewan, where the proportion of people over 65 closely resembles that of countries like Sweden (Health and Welfare Canada 1982, 1). The fact that small towns in Canada experienced the fastest growth in demographic aging during the 60s and 70s was due, in part, to the exodus of young people during this period.

Language and Ethnicity

The older population was more likely than those under 65 to speak a language other than French or English at home. This is not surprising, given the historical pattern of immigration to Canada. Census figures show that people in the older age groups who did not speak one of the two major languages of Canada at home were concentrated in the Prairie provinces and the Territories (Health and Welfare Canada 1983, 28). Ethnic groups found to have proportions of elderly above the Canadian average are British, Czech and Slovak, Finnish, Jewish, Russian, Hungarian, Polish and Scandinavian (Health and Welfare Canada 1982, 2; Health and Welfare Canada

FIGURE 3.2

PARTIAL AGE PYRAMIDS FOR THE POPULATION AGED 65 AND OVER, CANADA, 1961, 1981, 2001 AND 2021

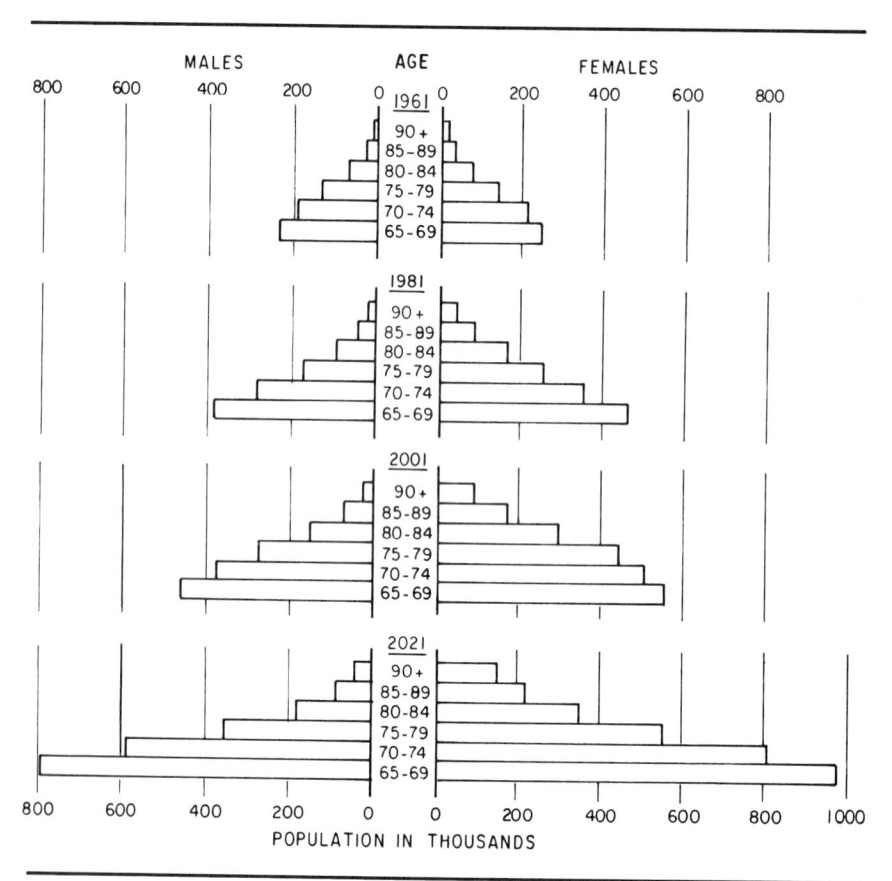

SOURCE: Canada. 1983. *Fact Book on Aging in Canada*. Ottawa: Minister of Supply and Services Canada. P. 19.

1983, 30). Only 3.5 percent of Canada's native peoples are in the age group 65 and over (Health and Welfare Canada 1983, 32).

Size of the Older Population

Dramatic shifts are occurring within the older population itself; it is also experiencing demographic aging. Figure 3.2 shows the trends in aging in this older group. In 1961, the proportion over 80 years old of the population 65 years and above was negligible. By 1981, it had grown to almost one-fifth of the total older population. By 2001, it is projected, the group 80 years and over will become almost 25 percent of the older population. Among the very old (80+) in 1981, 81 percent resided in large urban centres (Health and Welfare Canada 1982, 1). More of those above the age of 80 tend to speak English at home than those 65 and over (Health and Welfare Canada 1983, 28). It is most often those over the age of 75 who require health care, nursing home care and/or hospitalization. As this group grows, health care costs are likely to rise.

CONCLUSION

In this chapter, we examined Canada's place within the world picture, with respect to demographic aging. Second, the historical picture of population aging in Canada was analyzed. Third, a few selected contemporary patterns of aging in Canada were described briefly. It should be clear that whether or not one sees Canada as old depends very much on the perspective taken. It depends as well on the reference point used. Clearly, Canada is getting older, but this is by no means an abrupt change from past trends. If anticipated, the needs of tomorrow's older population can be accommodated. We can also adjust to the requirements and changes of a country whose population growth has diminished or stopped.

CHAPTER 4

CONTEMPORARY ISSUES AND CONCERNS ABOUT POPULATION AGING

Of the many social issues raised by demographic aging and associated changes, a few can be seen as focal points around which other concerns cluster. Several of these issues will be highlighted in this chapter, including the advent of zero population growth, the economic implications of supporting a growing older population, the possible effects on mobility and various kinds of opportunities (such as the opportunity to marry in an aging population), and the particular problems women face in an aging population. Discussion will emphasize the most contentious and complex issues, rather than attempting to be comprehensive. Perspectives first discussed in Chapter 2 will be applied here to reveal different dimensions of the issues discussed. Issues addressed in this chapter raise important policy questions as well. These will be addressed further in Chapter 5. (Many of the concerns introduced here will be discussed in considerably more detail in subsequent books in the Aging Series.)

THE ADVENT OF ZERO POPULATION GROWTH

As we have seen earlier, it is not so much declining mortality or lengthened life expectancy that cause a population to age, as it is declining fertility. In this chapter, we will examine the recent research findings that somewhat alter the picture. However, suffice it to say for now that demographic aging is generally a function of decreased numbers of young entrants to the population. This results in the older population representing a greater portion of the total — hence a demographically aging population.

Declining fertility, although not the only cause of population aging, is a central contributor. Concern with demographic aging focusses in part on the causally linked shifts occurring at the base and at the apex of the population pyramid. At the same time as the elderly are comprising a larger proportion of total population, the birth rate is declining so fewer youths are present in the population. A population that is aging in demographic terms, therefore, is one moving toward zero population growth. To analyze some of the social, economic and political outcomes and concerns associated with the advent of little or no population growth is to focus on a central issue of population aging.

Zero Population Growth and Mortality

A commonly held, but false, impression is that zero population growth is a relatively recent phenomenon. Many of us have the notion, often supported by vivid statistical graphs, that population growth until very recent times has been steady, consistent and positive. The recent emergence of a slowing rate of growth with the possibility of either zero growth or population decline in the future then is perceived as a break with the historical pattern. In fact, there is nothing new about zero population growth. Throughout human history there have been periods of no population growth interspersed with growth periods (Clark 1967). For example, the world's population failed to grow significantly prior to 1700, and in fact decreased by some two-fifths in the 1400s as a result of the Black Plague (Spengler 1978, 7). These periods of zero growth correspond to periods of high mortality, during which large numbers of infants and small children succumbed to death. In these times, which according to Clark's historical account prevailed until the seventeenth century, mortality rather than fertility was the determining factor in population growth. When sustained population growth began in earnest in the nineteenth century, it was due again to mortality factors rather than changes in fertility. Declines in mortality enabled many people to live longer, but the effect of declining mortality was particularly striking on infants and young children. Instead of succumbing to diseases of childhood, they lived to reproductive age and beyond. In this way, then, declining mortality had a double effect on population growth. More people survived at all ages, but greater numbers of children lived sufficiently long to reproduce.

Although zero population growth is not new, it is easy to understand why it may not be welcome. Its historical association with high levels of mortality may make us fear the end of humanity. For instance, in the Great Depression years, concerns were expressed frequently about depopulation (Beaujot and McQuillan 1982, 75). Population growth tends to be associated with health in the public mind — as the phrase, "a healthy rate of growth," suggests. Conversely, lack of population growth may be seen as unhealthy.

In this almost primordial linking of zero population growth to death, some important factors tend to be overlooked. For example, present-day zero population growth is not linked to mortality in the same way as in the past. Rather, it is declining fertility that contributes most to the advent of zero population growth today. Another often overlooked factor is that in many parts of the world, including North America, slowing population growth may be more conducive to collective health and survival than continuing high rates of growth. This is because many of the world's nonrenewable resources are being depleted at a fairly rapid rate, because of the affluent lifestyle of many North Americans and Western Europeans.

Paradoxically, the approaching zero population growth rate for many societies in the 1980s and 1990s may actually result in an increase in the death rate. This is due to the shifting age structure of the population; it has nothing to do with the historical relationship of high mortality and zero growth. When death rates declined precipitously in Western Europe and North America in the nineteenth and early twentieth centuries, biological life spans did not increase significantly. What happened instead was that a much greater proportion of people reached their full life expectancy. When an increased percentage of the population is composed of older people, even if the actual probability of dying remains low, the death rate tends to increase, because more people are close to their biological maximum life span. When deaths are aggregated per 1,000 population, the death rate tends to be higher in aging populations with high life expectancies.

The Link between Population Growth and Economic Growth

Apprehension about the advent of zero population growth is not simply a function of its historical association with mortality increase. Population growth has been linked, in the past as well as now, with economic growth. An increasing population means new workers, new consumers, viable mobility prospects (as older people retire and are replaced by younger people), and generally high levels of prosperity. This, of course, assumes constant or growing rates of employment, controlled inflation and no major catastrophes such as war, famine or plague. Conversely, economic growth and vitality have been associated with periods of population growth or with demographically increasing societies. However, there is also a question of balance, at least according to many theories of the relationship between economic and population growth. A rate of population growth that is too high, such as in many countries of Asia and Latin America today, is thought to thwart economic growth. In situations of limited economic resources, population growth may be a liability. Once economic viability is established, however, it can be maintained by population growth.

A great fear in advanced industrial societies is that both demographic and economic growth limits may be reached in the very near future, if they have not already been reached. In capitalist societies, growth is essential to the economy. It is necessary for producers of goods to find ever-greater markets for their products. This is why so much money goes into advertising and, in essence, creating the "need" in consumers for goods they never dreamed they needed before.

A society that is approaching zero population growth and at the same time aging is not a welcome prospect to many businessmen and politicians in Western capitalist countries. Older people tend to be less active consumers than younger people. This is due, in part, to the fact that they have already accumulated most of what they need. But it is also because they can be less easily convinced than younger people to follow the latest fads in cars, fashions, cosmetics, music, foods, and other consumer goods. An aging population may thus be seen as an economic spectre, not because it will be a challenge to meet its needs, but because of the fear that without population growth, economic growth and vitality will no longer be sustained.

Of course, a realistic approach to the problem of slowed economic growth due to zero population growth may be to provide the older population with sufficient disposable income as well as consumer goods appropriate to their age group, so they can continue to be viable consumers. This proposal obviously flies in the face of present-day concerns about where to find the money to meet the economic, social and health care needs of retired people. It also runs counter to recent government proposals, in both Canada and the U.S., to reduce pension benefits by de-indexing pensions from the cost of living. However, increasing pensions might ultimately provide an economic solution to what must be seen as an essentially economic problem. In providing better pensions to retired people, the economy, even in the advent of zero population growth, would remain viable. With the increased autonomy and enhanced self-esteem created by having a decent standard of living, older people might actually require less health care and social assistance than they do now. They would no longer feel like burdens on society. In the short run this solution might be more expensive, but in the longer run, it could not only actually save money but, more importantly, enhance the quality of later life and the morale of older people.

A second approach to the issue of zero population growth in an aging society would be to recognize that limits to economic growth might be approaching, regardless of what is occurring demographically. Even without zero population growth, markets cannot expand infinitely. Keynes himself recognized that, at some point, zero or negative economic growth must occur (Spengler 1978, 19). Although disturbing, this may be an expected and natural outcome of a capitalist economy. Barring the discovery of enormous markets for our products on other planets or in other solar systems, it makes sense to see markets as limited, in spite of the contemporary expansion of some markets in modernizing countries of the Third World. It may be, then, that the limits to growth are induced by economic rather than demographic processes. If this is so, viewing the advent of zero population growth or the aging of society as the *cause* of economic decline may be a case of misplaced causality.

Some evidence for the above argument may be found in contemporary Canadian trends. The economic growth rate of the 1980s seems to have slowed, in fits and starts perhaps, but slowed nonetheless. High levels of inflation and unemployment are signs of the economic problems of our times. Reduced profit margins in many industries and businesses, as well as closures and bankruptcies attest to the slowing of economic growth. University graduates trying to find a job in the mid-1980s quickly recognize that all is not well economically, despite the glowing forecasts of financial analysts. Although Canada's population has been aging for over a century, the biggest surge in growth of the aging population is not expected to occur until 2010 or so. This is when the first phase of the baby boom generation will enter retirement age. Not until 2025 will almost all people of the baby boom generation be in the retirement years, assuming retirement continues to occur around the age of 65. To claim that today's economic problems are caused by population aging or zero population growth seems too simplistic in light of the fact that economic problems have *preceded* the advent of an actual acceleration in population aging.

Aging, Zero Population Growth, and Level of Economic Development

It has been clearly established in previous chapters that the primary contributor to demographic aging is declining fertility. In societies such as Canada, however, which are approaching zero population growth and have very high life expectancies, it is necessary to reexamine and specify this statement further. The dynamic relationship between declining fertility, increased longevity, population growth, and demographic aging shifts somewhat in these circumstances. This is a relatively recent discovery and warrants particular attention.

There is no doubt that in the past, and even today in most societies, population aging was, for the most part, a direct consequence of fertility reduction. Mortality effects were negligible and, if anything, tended to make populations more youthful by reducing the probability of dying among the very young. In the most developed countries, such as Canada, however, where life expectancy is 70 years or more and where fertility declines have occurred to such a degree that zero population growth is imminent, the effects of fertility on aging may not be so straightforward and simple.

Among the few societies in the world where life expectancy is very high, the probability of dying in youth is very small and is often due to accident or misfortune rather than causes that are more easily affected by social improvement programs. This means that any further mortality declines, to the extent that they occur, must differentially affect the older population. The biological life span of the older group is not being extended, as many people think. Rather, the probability of reaching full life expectancy is being increased. This suggests that population aging may occur in several ways, with different causes and different consequences in various types of societies. Here, two types will be discussed: aging at the base (i.e., chipping away at the bottom of the population pyramid) resulting from fertility declines, and aging at the apex (i.e., actual growth at the top of the population pyramid) resulting from mortality declines. In Canada today, it is largely aging at the apex that is occurring. The two types of aging have rather different consequences in terms of the economic burden created.

Friedlander and Klinov-Malul (1980) have examined three situations of population change in order to compare the dynamic relationships between population growth rates, economic burden, fertility, mortality and aging. Their results are briefly summarized here. In the first situation, life expectancy is held constant over time while fertility declines. As a consequence, the proportion of young people declines while the proportion of working age and 65 years and over remains constant. After many years of low fertility, the proportion of the older group relative to the total begins to increase. This is accompanied by a very small change in the relative size of the working age population and a significant decline in dependent children. The result is that the overall economic burden is actually reduced. The United States might be an example of a country experiencing such a pattern.

In the second instance, fertility remains virtually unchanged while life expectancy increases. This results, according to Friedlander and Klinov-Malul (1980, 52–53), in a simultaneous increase in the overall rate of population growth and a relative decline in the proportion of working age population. The latter occurs because both the younger group (through constant fertility) and the older group (through increased longevity) gain, relative to the working age population. This situation leads to a greater economic burden for the working population as the population ages, since both the proportion of old and the proportion of young increase. Many African and Asian countries would be examples of this pattern.

The third situation allows for a simultaneous decline in fertility and an increase in life expectancy. This may be the case in Canada. However, Canada's fertility decline has been pronounced and prolonged, while recent increases in life expectancy have not been significant. In this case, there is a sizeable diminishing of the younger population relative to the total population, an increase in the older group, and a shrinking of the working age population. In terms of aging, this situation is the one in which aging occurs most rapidly and reaches the highest levels. Here, population growth moves toward zero at a faster rate than in the other two situations, although not much faster than in the first instance. Given the fact, however, that the burden of children also declines, it is not clearly the case that the increase in the older population will result in an increased economic burden. As Friedlander and Klinov-Malul (1980, 55) admit, however, this situation likely will be associated with a decline in per capita consumption and with greater dependency by the older population on pension income.

Changing Attitudes toward Population in the Advent of Zero Growth

The prospect of zero population growth, because of its historical association with mortality and its modern-day association with economic stagnation, is frightening to many people, as it was during the Great Depression (Beaujot and McQuillan 1982, 75). They envision an increase in death rates, even as health conditions continue to improve, a growing economic burden of pensions and health care for the elderly, a society that spiritually and socially lacks the possibility of rejuvenation, and an increasingly conservative political outlook (Day 1978). Attitudes, whether based on solid understandings or ungrounded apprehensions, can have enormous implications. The classic sociological insight on this comes from W. I. Thomas (1923) when he noted that what people believe to be true can have very real consequences, whether or not what they believe is in fact true. A good example of this is when bank account holders believe so strongly in the bank's insolvency that they all withdraw their funds, thereby rendering the bank insolvent. Similarly, people's perceptions and apprehensions about the advent of a zero population growth society can have real consequences. Believing that aging will have negative effects may bring on fear of aging and of the elderly. We consequently might expect less from older people. It is for this reason that attitudes toward population aging and the advent of zero growth are of fundamental importance and concern to policy makers.

In discussions of population aging, it is often overlooked that aging is the *unintended* consequence of people's actual decisions. Population aging is often perceived, even by demographic analysts at times, as something that happens randomly, like a tornado or a hurricane. In fact, there are further similarities in this analogy, in that people brace themselves for the onslaught of population aging in much the same way that they might brace themselves for a hurricane, thinking that they are helpless to protect themselves from the potential consequences of the event. There is a considerable time lag between the decline in family size and the point where the effects of population aging are felt, but there is a clear link. It should be emphasized here that we are not saying that couples who decide to have two children instead of three, or none instead of one, are *calculating* that, 50 years or so in the future, the population will experience the consequences of their collective actions. It must be added, however, that individual decisions about the utility or desirability of children, taken collectively, do have unintended population consequences many years hence.

Childbearing decisions within a society are not taken in isolation, even though they may manifest our most intimate feelings of love, security, devotion to God or humanity and/or belief in oneself, or one's marriage. These decisions occur in a context that is determined, to a large extent, by societal attitudes toward children and family, but also by fluctuating/cyclical social attitudes on labour force needs and population growth. Take, for example, a finding from a fertility survey conducted in Edmonton, Alberta in the mid-1970s (McDaniel 1984b). In this survey, respondents were asked whether they felt concerned about the world's rate of population growth. Some correlation was found between level of concern and lower family size expectations. Of course, some individuals who were very concerned also wanted to have large families. On average, however, people who were most concerned about the rate of population growth wanted smaller families. This finding reveals the existence of a tie between attitudes toward population growth and actual reproductive aspirations and behaviours.

The degree of the fertility decline of the 1970s and 1980s in Canada is unprecedented. Demographers, fooled for a time by the precipitous drop in family size, thought until very recently (1983 or 1984) that low fertility was a temporary phenomenon that would turn around with a change in some unidentified conditions (women's rights, economic situation, belief in the future, etc.). Demographers, clearly, have been forced to accept the fact that the low fertility of Canadians during the past decade and a half is not an anomaly, but a true expression of their preferences (Grindstaff 1985). What factors have produced this historically unprecedented low fertility remain somewhat uncertain, but women's roles, economic difficulties, availability of choice in childbearing and a changed attitude to population growth seem to play a role (Grindstaff 1975; McDaniel 1984a).

What is important to understand is that it was changing attitudes toward population growth that, to some extent, precipitated the currently low birth rates being experienced in North America and most of Europe. These attitudes are grounded in genuine concern about the rate of population growth and resource utilization in the world, and in concern about the costs, either in actual money or in lost opportunities, of rearing a child in these times. Whatever the reasons, there is obviously an attitudinal context in which the advent of zero population growth and an aging population must be seen. There may be a lag, and the consequences may be unintended, but the prospect of zero population growth and an aging population actually *grew out of* the changed attitudes and collective decisions of people. A society characterized by the prospect of population aging and zero population growth resulting from deliberately reduced fertility may be one that is prepared to accept the challenges created by these changes. A society facing zero growth because of lack of control over mortality may be swept up in forces that it cannot control, and thus may be unable to adequately plan its future.

There is little question that many industrialists, business people and politicians are concerned about the advent of a zero population growth society. To them it means a decline in potential markets, limited numbers of new workers, escalating demands of retiring workers for decent pension plans, decreasing opportunities for upward mobility, and an increasing imbalance in growth rates between the developed world and the Third World.

However, there are also positive attitudes toward zero population growth in an aging society. These positive attitudes may be part of the motivation behind declining fertility. Environmental pollution and resource depletion could become less of a problem with zero population growth (provided consumers do not squander resources or recklessly deal with waste). A population that is not growing tends to have a large proportion of working age people relative to those who are dependent. Mothers with smaller families have greater opportunities to participate in work, thereby increasing the numbers of people who are economically active. The low youth dependency ratio also permits families to save more money (Overbeek 1980, 152). Since demographic demands are diminished in a no-growth population, more economic resources are available for investment. Provided that per capita consumption does not increase too dramatically, the potential investment capital available with zero population growth should be increased.

These benefits of zero population growth seem to be embedded in the consciousness of the cohorts who decided to have fewer children. Yet, the disadvantages of no growth, which clearly exist, seem to be receiving most of the media attention. The result is a further shaping of public opinion in such a way that zero growth and an aging population are feared and viewed with apprehension. This can result in a siege mentality on the part of the public — fearing that the economic pie is shrinking, people demand more and more for themselves before it vanishes. This attitude, not well grounded in fact, is remarkably similar to the attitude that creates bank insolvency, as mentioned earlier. Fear that the bank is insolvent causes it to be so. Thus, negative attitudes toward zero population growth may create further problems, rather than solutions.

ECONOMIC CONCERNS IN AN AGING POPULATION

In this section, some of the general economic challenges posed by Canada's changing age composition are examined. These include economic and demographic dependency burdens, productivity effects, and the distribution of wealth among groups and between private and public sources. Issues of social mobility will be considered later in the chapter, while the policy implications of these economic issues will be discussed in Chapter 5.

At heart, concerns about an aging population are economic. The issues become political and social at times, but even then they can be said to have economic roots. Davis and van den Oever's (1981) image of emerging conflicts between young and old, which result in what they call an inter-generational "class struggle," can be seen, by virtue of the terms used, as conflict over the allocation of scarce wealth.

Shifting Economic and Demographic Dependency Burdens

So much alarm has been generated about the supposed impending surge of older people in the population that this group has been termed "a tidal wave" (Calvert 1977, 4). Fears have been expressed about the possibility of a taxpayer's revolt in the face of the impossible burden of ever-increasing pensions (Ridler 1979; Patterson 1980; both citing Calvert 1977). Others have suggested the possibility of inter-generational warfare (Davis and van den Oever 1981) or economic stagnation resulting from a combination of zero population growth and decreased productivity (Myles 1982). The "scare" imagery has at least five assumptions: 1) that growth in the proportion of older people in the population is new and somehow unexpected; 2) that the levels of older people in the population will be so high as to be unprecedented (hence leading to inter-generational warfare, and other social problems); 3) that an increase in the proportion of older people means an increased burden for those of working age; 4) that an aging population cannot produce a reduced dependency burden; and 5) that growth in the older population necessarily has negative economic consequences. All these assumptions about the nature of demographic aging and about the past and future of aging in Canada are fallacious.

It was clearly shown in Chapter 3 that the first two assumptions are incorrect. Canada has been experiencing population aging since its inception. There is nothing new or unexpected in Canada's experiencing growth in the older population. Thus, today's alarmism about population aging seems overblown and somewhat misguided. Similarly, it was shown in Chapter 3 that, relative to other advanced industrial countries, Canada is demographically rather young. Our demographic future has been experienced by several countries of Western Europe already, without economic collapse or inter-generational warfare.

The third assumption mentioned above is a rather interesting one. Many analysts, both in the media and in academia, take this view — that as the elderly make up a larger part of the total population, it will become more difficult for the working population to support them. The thinking, often made explicit, is that the growth of the older population tends to deplete the ranks of the working population. Sometimes this is expressed in terms of a solid analysis, as in the case of Ridler (1979, 534), who notes that the old age dependency ratio will double in Canada from 1971 to 2031. Sometimes the statement is more alarmist. For example, Calvert (1977, 5) sees the declining birth rate as taking "lethal aim at the capacity of the working population to support the older sections of the population."

What is overlooked in focussing on old age dependency is that the dependency burden consists of the young as well as the old, both groups presumably dependent on the working age population. In an analysis of the overall dependency burden, Ridler states that the cost of an aging population is offset by the declining burden posed by the young. In fact, his calculations indicate that the total dependency rate does not reach the level it was in 1976 until 2071 (Ridler 1979, 535).

Calvert, cited above, takes the view that dependency ratios *per se* do not adequately tap economic dependency, which may be true. His position, clearly articulated in his 1977 book, *Pensions and Survival: The Coming Crisis of Money and Retirement*, is that youth dependency is fundamentally different from old age dependency. While people might be more than willing to bear the economic costs of dependent children, these costs are borne largely because they are individualized. That is, one pays the costs of raising one's own children. Costs of supporting a dependent older population, however, are more often public. It is for this reason, argues Calvert (1977, 24), that total dependency ratio is not a compelling measure of economic burden. Therefore, he maintains, the ratio of the older population to the working age population is the crucial economic measure.

Several researchers, in addition to Ridler, have shown that an increase in the proportion of older people in the population is not likely to lead to an increased dependency burden. Denton and Spencer (1979) project dependency ratios for Canada until 2001, based on six sets of assumptions. They conclude that, even with the projection that shows the largest increases in dependency ratio, the proportion of total dependents in the future will be lower in Canada than it was in 1956, 1961 or 1966. Myles (1982, 40) concludes that "the relative size of the working age population in 2031 will be almost identical to today's level and in fact will increase between now and 2010." He predicts that the overall dependency burden in Canada will decrease during the next thirty years and then return to current levels. A similar conclusion is reached by Foot (1982, 143).

It is important to emphasize that dependency ratios do not measure actual economic dependency and may, as a result, be subject to misinterpretation and even create confusion about the future burden of an aging population. Nonetheless, it is clear that an increase in the proportion of older people in the population does *not* necessarily mean an increased burden for those of working age. An aging population can actually result in a *reduced* dependency burden.

The fifth assumption of the alarmist position is that growth in the older population has negative economic consequences. This point encompasses many of the issues and arguments raised earlier about zero population growth. It also relates to issues of productivity and creativity (to be discussed later in this chapter). In terms of the dependency burden, a few points should be made about the possible consequences of growth in the older age groups. First, not all people over the age of 65 are economically dependent, just as many who are of working age do not actually contribute. Some older people continue to work either full-time or part-time. Others have sufficient money of their own, or from their extended family, that they do not rely on public pensions. Still others have sufficient private pension funds. Second, the increased dependency of the older population can be offset by the declining size of the younger age groups. This may require an innovative redistribution of funds, but it is possible to utilize some monies previously spent on children to provide for older people. Third, the older population may actually contribute to the economy by consuming more in terms of travel, vacation homes, meals eaten in restaurants, professional services, etc., than was previously imagined. This is especially likely for the future cohorts of older people who have been part of, or influenced by, the consumer-oriented baby boom generation (i.e. born between 1946 and 1960). So it would appear that the assumption that growth in the older population necessarily means negative economic consequences may not be justified.

Productivity and Creativity Concerns

Closely related to issues of demographic and economic dependency are concerns about levels of productivity and creativity in an aging population. To some degree, these must be treated as separate issues, although they are both tied to our collective fears about what it might mean to live in a society that is not growing and rejuvenating. (Issues addressed above as part of the discussion of dependency burdens, such as whether or not older people are actually economically dependent, will not be reconsidered here.)

Implicit in any discussion of the relationship between productivity and aging are questions of *ageism*, a term coined in the late 1960s by Robert Butler, Director of the U.S. National Institute of Aging. Butler (1969, 244) defines ageism as a "process of systematic stereotyping, of discriminating against people because they are old." The supposition or fear that an older society will be less productive economically relates partly to the changed ratio of working age population to the older, presumably non-working, population, but it relates as well to beliefs and stereotypes about the age at which productivity peaks and declines.

Concerns about possible declines in productivity as a population ages are not new. Graebner (1980) credits a Canadian, William Osler, with the dubious distinction of being the first (in 1905) to articulate the uselessness of men over forty. Osler's focus was on societal achievements, which he claimed would be about the same if all efforts of people over 40 were excluded. It is clear that serious consequences for meeting the challenges of an aging society can result from this kind of attitude. If it is believed, even partially, that older people are useless, there may be an inclination to see them as a burden, whether or not they actually are in economic terms.

Demographers, historians, economists and psychologists have echoed concern about the decline in productivity that could result from an aging population. Indeed, apprehension has even been expressed about the supposedly limited contributions that can be made by those over 35 (!) (Notestein *et al.* 1944). Innovation and creativity are thought to diminish because of the slowed reaction times and rigidity of thought among older people (see literature cited by McPherson 1983, 204-205). Creative energy, perceived as the prerogative of the young, would decline in an aging society, thereby contributing further to diminished productivity (Sauvy 1948). While some readers might conclude from the dates of the older research materials cited here that this point of view is outmoded, it should be noted that many of these sentiments were expressed in a rather recent report by the Economic Council of Canada (1979). They are also expressed on occasion in Canada's newspapers and news magazines. This view has no scientific basis. But it is not only science that affects and determines people's beliefs or biases. In fact, scientific evidence has had limited success in eliminating racial prejudice or sexism, so it might be expected that biases about the elderly will also persist to some degree.

Concern about declining productivity and creativity in an aging population can be divided into two parts. The first is the economic or structural concern that sees an aging population as less capable of producing wealth than a younger population. The second is more individual and psychological and therefore of less interest in this book. It suggests that older people have declining abilities, so that if there are more of them in a population, the average productivity of that population will decrease. Associated with this concern is the view that living in a society made up of people at the end of their lives might have a depressing effect on the spirit, creativity and productivity of younger people as well (Calvert 1977). Of course, these concerns are not mutually exclusive, but interpenetrating, in that it is thought that individual declines in productivity cause lowered work force productivity when the population ages. Conversely, the burden of supporting a large, economically dependent older population is thought to sap the productivity and creativity of the working age population. What is the evidence for each of these concerns?

With respect to the aging population's potential (or not) to produce wealth, the evidence is clear and compelling. Examples from both history and today's most aged societies indicate that production of wealth does not decline with demographic aging. The historical evidence, in fact, seems to suggest that the opposite is true. The most rapid economic growth period in history corresponds directly to that period in which rapid demographic aging was occurring. Similarly, contemporary "old" societies such as Sweden, Germany or Austria reveal little evidence of economic decline in response to their changing age structure. In fact, these societies seem to be thriving economically. As well, Sweden stands out as an example of a country that, although old in demographic terms, is often cited as one of the most progressive countries in the world. In terms of health care, lowered rates of infant mortality, equality of opportunity and rights for women, Sweden seems creative and vital indeed. In comparison with younger countries like Canada or Australia, many of Europe's oldest societies are doing well both economically and socially. Factors other than median age, or the proportion of the population above the age of 65, therefore seem important to productivity.

With respect to concern about the declining abilities of older people, recent research has revealed that some of what was previously thought to be rigidity of thought resulting from aging, has now been found to be a function of cohort and historical factors. It might be, for example, that earlier tests were done in such a way as to be biased in favour of younger people's cognitive styles, because the standards are often based on the responses of university students. Creativity is known to peak at different ages in different fields of endeavour and in different societies. In a society in which older people are devalued, they may be less likely to have the *opportunity* to be productive or creative.

Wealth Distribution

Associated with the belief that an aging population will result in diminished productivity, creativity and wealth in Canada is the notion that older persons in the population take from society more than they give. We have seen some of the ways in which this view rests on biases and unfounded assumptions. However, part of this concern stems from the belief that most, if not all, of the increasing numbers of older people, particularly women, will constitute a burden on the working population in terms of pensions, health care and welfare services.

Embedded in this concern are several aspects of the North American value system, which merit brief attention here. The notion exists that every person should be in charge of himself/herself and economically self-supporting. Dependency in the economic sense, or even in the physical sense, is seen to render a person childlike. Rugged individualism is valued, although perhaps to a lesser extent in Canada than in the birthplace of the concept, the United States. Lastly, there is the notion that the person who controls the money is entitled to say how it should be spent, or, to put it colloquially, "He who pays the piper calls the tune." However, these values are somewhat tempered in their application. For example, the idea that everyone should be economically self-sufficient is not applied with such rigour to children and married women with young children at home. Despite the belief that dependency is not ideal, parents regularly extend support to their adult children and their older parents, without regret or resentment. Rugged individualism is not insisted upon when people are in need, out of work or without hope. The long-established Canadian social welfare system is intended for such extreme situations, but it also provides a guaranteed minimal level of health care, unemployment insurance and pension to all. The belief that the person who pays should call the tune is ignored in the case of transfer payments from government to people, or from one government agency to another. This money is considered as well spent if it goes from those who do not need it, i.e. most taxpayers, to the minority who need it more, i.e. mothers with dependent children, the ill, pensioners, etc.

The importance of examining these Canadian values is to show that they are far from homogeneous. There is a long-standing tradition in Canada of public taxation for the benefit of everyone. It is not clear that supporting pensioners, even a growing number of them, contradicts this value in any way. Many pensioners would no doubt be supported, in large measure, by private pension plans. Others are seen as having made their contribution by a lifetime of working and/or raising children. The notion that older people are taking, through receipt of pensions, rather than giving is not likely to be a widely held view in Canada. The recent outcry by retirees about the 1985 Canadian government proposal to de-index pensions received considerable support from a constituency of working age people. The likelihood of a taxpayers' revolt in response to the growing burden of pensions does not seem strong in Canada.

As we have seen, there is no doubt that the number and proportion of people over the age of 65 will increase in Canada in the future. However, it is also clear that the total number of dependents will decrease as long as the birth rate remains low. In actual economic terms then, the dependency burden will not increase. However, the nature of economic dependency will move from private support of young dependents by their own families to public support of the elderly. Funds previously allocated to the raising of children within the family could be transferred to providing pensions and health care for the older population. This, however, will not happen automatically. In a climate of fear and apprehension about the growing "burden" of the elderly, people may be reluctant to switch private funds to public sources through, for example, increased taxes. However, if a carefully implemented program of education and planning were to be undertaken by the government, universities and the private sector, the shift could be more easily made. In situations of necessity, Canadians are willing to assist their neighbours, family members and strangers. Books such as this one and subsequent ones in the series on Aging could aid in such a task of education. To dismiss the possibility of supporting the growing older population in Canada as impossible is to underestimate the Canadian people, as well as the Canadian value system.

MOBILITY AND OPPORTUNITY STRUCTURE IN AN AGING POPULATION

Individual chances for social mobility tend to be best in an economy that is growing. A growing economy is often associated with a growing population. An increasing number of social scientists (Denton and Spencer 1982; Dooley and Gottschalk 1985; Easterlin 1978 and 1980; Freeman 1979) have been searching for links between shifts in age structure (the movement of population out of some age categories and into others) and declining mobility opportunities.

It makes sense to think that the demographic structure can have a bearing on all aspects of social life. Clearly, competition for scarce resources (including jobs, promotions, classrooms, spouses, houses, pensions and health care) is, to some extent, a function of the size of the group of competitors. As well, of course, access depends on the health and priorities of the economy. However, to step from this realization to the idea that shifting age structure is the driving force behind many social and institutional changes in a giant step.

The Age Structure Argument

There has been a long tradition, in both economics and demography, of analyzing the effects of shifting age structure on economic opportunity. Often these analyses are speculative, i.e. what would happen to the supply of workers/consumers in a situation of marked population aging? Sometimes analysts attempt to quantify the effects of population aging on mobility chances. Analysts such as Easterlin (1978; 1980) have focussed on the more general effects of a shifting age structure on crime, divorce, scholastic achievement, etc. The commonality in these diverse approaches is that age structure is seen as the basis of social change.

To clarify, let us give a few examples. Imagine that you were born in Canada around the mid-1920s. Say you were a mediocre student with no outstanding career aspirations. You decide, for lack of anything better, to take a job as a salesperson in the bottled food industry. By the late 1940s, when you are still employed in the firm but not a rising star, the baby boom arrives. Suddenly, through no effort on your part or even on the part of the firm, business takes off as demand for baby food rapidly grows. Because you were born at a time of low birth rates, there is little competition from people in your age group for positions. You quickly rise to the position of Vice-President (Sales) in a very successful firm. Thus, shifts in age structure, cohort size in this instance, can profoundly affect the mobility prospects of a person who, because of his or her background, training and motivation might not expect to rise to such a position, and thereby experience the accompanying social benefits and lifestyle.

A second example may be closer to home for many university students of the late 1980s. You were born into a small generation that immediately followed a huge generation, that of the baby boom. In order to compete for jobs in an often flooded job market, members of the baby boom generation stayed in school for a long time or remained unemployed. Many of these people, in their late twenties to mid-thirties in 1985, are now competing for jobs with recent university graduates. Some of those born in the baby boom generation have marketable skills, job experience and maturity. Because of their rocky employment histories, however, many are forced to work for less money than the average person their age, in order to have a job. In essence, these people are artificially "reducing" their age and competing directly with younger "baby bust" generation people. This age structure problem, compounded by a poor economy, makes for a somewhat dismal employment picture for people born in the 1960s and 1970s. This is not a function of their abilities, motivations or skills, but is due, at least in part, to the historical fact that they were born after the baby boom generation. Employment opportunities and life chances in this instance may be curtailed due to age structure shifts.

Employment opportunities are not the only aspect of life affected by demographic changes. A 1967 study by Akers found that age structure shifts even have implications for the marriage market. In an article provocatively entitled "On Measuring The Marriage Squeeze," Akers points out that men conventionally marry women who are, on average, two years younger than themselves. Where there is either an oversupply or undersupply of women in the marriageable categories, there might be a problem finding suitable mates. In the former case, it would be women who would either remain unmarried or find mates in other than ideal age categories. In the latter case, it would be men who would remain unmarried or marry women who are older, the same age or considerably younger than they. Thus, what might have been viewed as changing marriage mate preference can be seen as a consequence of shifts in age structure.

This way of analyzing social trends and patterns is alien to most of us. We are commonly taught that attitude shifts are the biggest source of social change in society. With our relatively individualistic values, we often consider that success or failure is due more to individual effort than to chance, or the size of one's birth cohort. The age structure argument requires us to think about how opportunities in our lives are influenced, either directly or indirectly, by population shifts.

Population Aging and Mobility

It is feared that population aging in our society might diminish mobility opportunities. This could work in a number of ways. Population aging, as we have seen, is often associated with low or no population growth, which in turn is thought to lead to limited economic growth. In such a society, individual opportunities for advancement might be curtailed. An aging population may also mean that increasing numbers of workers are clustered at the top of their pay scales or in positions from which they can no longer be promoted. Essentially, these highly paid workers are seen to block the channels of mobility for ambitious younger people. This may be particularly true for the baby boom generation, which collectively is not only the largest generation the Western world has ever experienced, but the best qualified in terms of education and training for high-prestige positions. Further, an aging population, it is argued, could so tax the economy that resources available for rewarding outstanding efforts (by promotions, raises or bonuses) might shrink.

In seeking an explanation for decreasing mobility chances in our society, aging population has become a focal point. However the supposed simplicity of the relationship between mobility and age structure distracts from the more complicated and perplexing economic problems of the day. Rather than accounting for diminished opportunity in terms of a recession, limited markets, or an unstable dollar, the explanation has been proposed that the problem is demographic. Policy-makers, taking their cue from this research orientation, tend to search for demographic answers to the problem of an aging population. Elevating the birth rate or increasing immigration levels have been suggested as solutions to an aging population (panel discussion of the Canadian Population Society, Montreal, June 1985). A further possibility is that policy-makers will do little to improve people's mobility chances because, they argue, the source of the problem rests with age structure, a not easily adjusted factor.

There have been a number of research efforts directed toward quantifying the effect of population aging on actual mobility prospects. One of the early studies predicting a decrease in promotion prospects with population aging was undertaken by Keyfitz (1973). He concludes, on the basis of a mathematical model, that the average office or factory worker would be delayed in reaching middle level positions by about 4.5 years, as the population growth rate declines from 2 percent to zero. Spengler (1978), in a book length study of the same problem, also discovers that mobility chances are diminished as a population ages. Easterlin (1978; 1980) bases his analysis on the crucial ratio of younger to older workers, a ratio he sees as "the driving force" behind many social trends. His analysis counters that of Keyfitz and Spengler in that he sees mobility prospects as increasing in the future, as the demand for younger workers increases and the supply decreases.

In Canada, Denton and Spencer (1982a) use a simulation model to project the relationship of age structure and promotion prospects into the future. They conclude that "there is ample reason to expect promotion prospects to be considerably worsened by population aging" (Denton and Spencer 1982a, 12). Specifically, they see mobility chances for the average male worker being slowed by 7.5 years in a zero growth situation, as compared with a hypothetical 4 percent growth situation. In a society with a "healthy" rate of population growth, the age structure is smooth, with few large and few small cohorts. Progress through the ranks is thus orderly and often age-linked. As a society ages, more people retain their positions longer, due to increased life expectancy and the greater proportion of people in the older labour force ages, thereby impeding the mobility of younger workers. McDaniel (1985) concludes that, for Canadian women, mobility prospects are diminished even more than for men in an aging society. This is because women often hold jobs in which age and promotions are uncorrelated. Older women returning to the work force often compete directly with young women. Women's promotion prospects are therefore blocked both by women, with whom they often compete, and by men, with whom women also compete but who often already hold the positions to which women want to be promoted.

It seems then that, even though much of the fear and apprehension about diminished mobility prospects with population aging is not well based in fact, there are some implications that cannot be overlooked. Promotion prospects in general decline with population aging, although this varies across occupations. The way in which diminished mobility prospects are interpreted socially, however, is very important. If mobility is seen as the legitimate reward for hard work and self-sacrifice, people may in fact be very disturbed by diminishing prospects. If, however, people find intrinsic rewards in the job or in their home lives, as recent data from quality of life surveys suggest, then the increasing time it may take to obtain promotions will matter less. For the baby boom generation, raised on stiff competition, changes in the years required to be promoted may not matter much. Often, acquiring and holding a job matters more.

THE PARTICULAR PROBLEMS OF WOMEN IN AN AGING SOCIETY

Women's life expectancy in Canada so exceeds men's that an aged population will be one with a significant imbalance by sex. In 1981, for example, there were 124 women for every 100 men aged 65–79. Among those 80 and over, there were 184 women to 100 men. By 2000, the comparable figures are expected to be 134 and 218 (Health and Welfare Canada 1983, 20). This means that by 2000, women aged 80 or more will outnumber men by more than 2 to 1. The problem is aggravated by the fact that women, on average, marry men who are slightly older. The older population of the future will be composed, to a larger extent than it is now, of widows.

Our discussion here will be confined to those issues arising out of population aging. (Other issues of women and aging will be discussed in detail in another book in the Aging Series.) Areas of concern include the social and economic implications of the sex ratio imbalance, the lifetime labour force participation and life cycle patterns of today's older women, and the larger, more symbolic issues of falsely equating aging with dependency. These concerns are not independent, but interrelated and overlapping.

The Predominance of Older Women

Population aging has meant the presence of increasing numbers of women in the population relative to men. There will be a large and increasing numerical dominance. When people in 1985 think of aging, they often first picture older women whose husbands have died. This image and the reality on which it is based have implications for how population aging is viewed by analysts, policy-makers and the public.

Women in Canada, as in most places in the world, outlive men. The gap between the life expectancy of men and that of women is largest in the most industrial parts of the world. In Canada in 1980-82, women aged 60 could expect to outlive men of the same age by almost five years (Statistics Canada 1984e, 16-19). Even at age 70, women can expect to live another 15.1 years and men only 11.6 years (Statistics Canada 1984e, 16-19). At birth, women's life expectancy in Canada in 1980-82 exceeds men's by 7.1 years (Statistics Canada 1984e, 84-85). This gap in life expectancy is actually widening, particularly at the older ages. Evidence of this is found in data from 1931, which reveal that at age 60, women in Canada outlived men by only 0.9 years (Denton, Feaver and Spencer 1980, 7). This means that the image of an older population made up largely of widows is not far off base. The fact that women tend, on average, to marry men at least two years older than themselves means that they can expect to live approximately ten years of their lives as widows.

Women who are entering old age, as we have come to define it, in 1985 in Canada were born around 1920. These women, with notable exceptions, were under stronger pressure than today's women to assume primary responsibility for the home and child care as their life work. Women reaching age 65 in 1985 were raising their children in the 1940s and 1950s, an era of heavy emphasis on the nuclear, surburban family with the father as sole breadwinner and the mother as homemaker. Although some of these women returned to the labour force after their children were grown up, many did not. If women worked during this period, they often worked in low-income, low-prestige and insecure jobs, which seldom came with pension packages. More of these women, compared to women in subsequent generations, face "retirement" as widows with no pensions except for the minimal one provided by the Canada Pension Plan.

For the next twenty years or so, many women facing retirement will likely be without dependable resources to assist them in old age (Phillips and Phillips 1983). Widows whose husbands had relatively good pension plans often experience the discontinuance of their husband's pension on his death. Lifetime homemakers, despite their contribution to society by raising children, keeping house, and providing for their husband's domestic needs, still are seen to have no right to pensions of their own in Canada (Canadian Advisory Council on the Status of Women, 1985). Although more of the women who were born in 1940 than those born in 1920 have worked outside the home at some time in their lives, they continue to work in jobs that have limited pension benefits (Dulude, 1981). The assumption still seems to be that women are dependent on their husbands and will be provided for by their husbands' pension plans. Unfortunately, this assumption seems to have little basis in fact. In the next few decades, these problems may be additionally compounded by increasing numbers of older women who are divorced, separated or never married.

The Confusion of Women's Dependency with Population Aging

The fact that the greatest number of older people are women and that many of these women are in dire financial straits (Dulude, 1981) due to their life cycle patterns of limited labour force participation suggests to some observers that population aging is, of necessity, problematic. Population aging is falsely defined as the source of the problem that places a burden on the public purse. In fact, the issue of women's dependency is a larger and different issue, not a problem of population aging. Women are more commonly found in the ranks of the poor or those on welfare, as well.

The association of old age with women's economic dependency or poverty may be a temporary one. As more women enter the labour force, public recognition may increase that women are not short-term workers but lifetime workers. This recognition, however, is likely to grow slowly since women have for many decades been viewed as a reserve labour pool in Western societies. The acknowledgement that women will work for years and face retirement will bring demands for new pension arrangements for women. It is to be hoped that, as a society, we will welcome such innovations as both necessary and just.

The false linkage of women's economic dependency in old age with population aging makes us all vulnerable to fears and apprehensions. We fear an aging population because we see ourselves as potentially old and poor. Further, women's social status tends to decline with age (Dulude 1981), in contrast to that of men, who grow in "character." This means that as a population ages, it becomes more and more characterized by old, poor women with low social status. It is easy to understand why fears and apprehensions are common, but misplaced, about living in an aging society. Providing for the economic needs of older women would go a long way to alleviate these fearful images.

CONCLUSION

In this chapter, a few of the more difficult and complex concerns and issues about population aging have been discussed. It must be mentioned again that other problems exist as well, such as issues of housing, health care, regional inequities, etc. It is hoped that the discussion of selected issues will stimulate a discussion of other issues. Population aging is an intricate and interwoven social phenomenon that touches all aspects of society. It raises important questions about our values, our hopes and our dreams, but also raises spectres of high taxes, death, poverty, dependency and limited creativity. The importance of these issues requires that serious attention be given to them in advance by practitioners, by researchers, by policy-makers and by the general public, all of whom face aging themselves.

CHAPTER 5

POLICY AND PROGRAM IMPLICATIONS OF POPULATION AGING

The issues and concerns raised in the previous chapter cannot be discussed only in the abstract. Nor can they be easily or readily dismissed simply because they may appear to be derived more from the realm of apprehension than from reality. Pragmatic attention, careful analysis and planned solutions are required. The alternative to planning for population aging is to acquiesce to our fears, thereby producing a self-fulfilling prophecy that population aging cannot be accommodated.

It is very difficult, if not impossible, to discuss the complex policy issues involved in population aging without reference to many areas that go beyond population aging. However, if population aging is seen by some, no matter how incorrectly, as reason for increasing concern about the future of Canadian society, it seems appropriate that this first book in the Aging Series touch on some basic policy issues raised by demographic aging. (These will of course be analyzed in considerably more detail in subsequent books in the series.)

This chapter is organized around five central areas of policy concern and analysis: the economy, retirement and work, health issues, housing and family, and education. (There will of course be some overlapping.) No attempt is made here to cover all the relevant policy issues; rather, the intent is to provoke thought, from a demographic perspective, about some of the central issues. This should generate discussion among students and policymakers about what can actually be done to meet the challenges posed by population aging.

It should be noted at the beginning that few public policies in Canada or elsewhere have been successful when directed at demographic goals such as reducing or increasing the birth rate (Stone and Marceau 1977, 57; Hawkins, 1985). The notable exception might be immigration policies. Even these, however, have sacrificed long-term planning (Stone and Marceau 1977, 57) to the imperatives of short-term economic need (Hawkins 1985). Thus, we have experienced in Canada the influx of large numbers of immigrants during certain decades. These immigrants, in the short run, contribute economically and demographically to the population. In the longer run, however, the shaping of immigration policy by short-term economic needs tends to produce an age-sex structure that exacerbates the effects of demographic aging. A less choppy flow of immigrants, from a demographic standpoint, would have been preferable.

ECONOMIC ISSUES

Population aging clearly affects all aspects of social, economic and political life. Much of the attention of researchers and policy-makers so far, however, has been devoted to the economic issues. In particular, as we saw in Chapter 4, the potential burden placed on workers by the increased elderly population has received much consideration. Shifting age structure, however one sees it, will create new policy challenges for Canadians, challenges that will require careful assessment and planned action, if we are to meet the emerging needs of an aging population. In this section, general economic policy issues in an aging society will be discussed. These issues include economic dependency and pensions, the economic problems faced by older women, and economic growth and productivity.

Economic Dependency and Pensions

Among the various policy issues connected with population aging, the most contentious seems to be the issue of pensions and economic dependency. This issue has generated the most concern about the prospects of an aging society (Calvert 1977; Myles 1984). It is, of course, intimately related to the limits to growth discussed in Chapter 4, as well as to fears that an aging society might be a less productive and progressive society.

Economic dependency is an essential public policy concern for at least two reasons. First, the continuation of population aging in Canada will see a reversal in the composition of the dependent population; it will go from being composed largely of youth to being increasingly composed of older people. Although this will not occur until well into the twenty-first century (see Figure 3.1), central policy questions are raised as monies and resources that primarily serve the young (such as education) are transferred to programs (such as pensions and health care) that serve the older members of society. In Canada, a significant proportion of dollars spent on education, health care and pensions are tax dollars, controlled by governments and therefore subject to public policy.

The second reason why economic dependency is a crucial issue of public policy stems from the organization of pension schemes today. Pension plans are based on the idea that each succeeding generation will support the preceding generation and will, in turn, be supported by the generation that follows (Myles 1984, 105). This means, for example, that pensions for the baby boom generation retiring in the 2020s and 2030s are expected to come from the pockets of the much smaller "baby bust" generation born in the

1970s and 1980s. Based on 1976 per capita payments, it is estimated that by 2021 in Canada the total amount required for public pensions will have increased by three and a half times (Stone and Fletcher 1980, 92). This estimate does not take inflation into account. It is not surprising, then, that economic dependency is often the central policy issue associated with population aging.

In the immediate future in Canada, there will be a reduced number (and proportion) of young people and an increased number (and proportion) of older people in the population. This will occur gradually until around 2021, at which time the number of older people will exceed the number of younger people in the population. Both history and simulation experiments (Denton and Spencer 1976) have demonstrated clearly that a sharp and prolonged decline in fertility will eventually result in a dramatic increase in the number of pensioners. This is occurring in Canada at present and will accelerate in the future. While this transition in the dependency burden is occurring, the proportion of the population of working age in Canada will remain fairly stable, in fact increasing in the near future, before it declines somewhat. This creates two advantages for Canadian policy-makers. One, they have a solid economic base on which to plan for the future, given the stability of the population proportion that is earning money. Second, they have a considerable period of time in which to adjust policies to better meet the economic requirements of an aging society.

To plan for an aging population requires a long-term perspective. The key to policy planning for an aging population in Canada seems to be that the *overall* dependency burden will not increase. Rather, the *nature* of the dependency will shift from youth to older people. Typically, analysts and futurologists compare the relative costs of public expenditures on the young with those on the old. Schools and vaccinations, they argue, cost less than one-third of what it costs to care for the old (Myles 1984, 107). In fact, the total cost, both private and public, of raising a child is estimated to be one-quarter to one-third *higher* than the cost of supporting an elderly person (Wander 1978). It could be argued, then, that the total cost of population aging, including both private and public expenditures, will be less than the actual cost of dependency in a youthful society.

Some analysts (Calvert 1977) acknowledge the economic advantage, in terms of dependency burden, of living in an aging society. Calvert and others, however, are very concerned about the prospect of increased taxes needed to pay for pensions and health care for the elderly. He states:

> ... whether it goes to pay pensions to elderly persons unknown, or paperwork and salaries of civil servants, or to buy battleships or monuments, it is still a tax, and it destroys the reward and incentive to work. Caring for and paying for one's own children has the very opposite effect on most parents. (Calvert 1977, 24)

Others (Foot 1982, 135) point out that the increasing tax burden on the working age population may be seen as unacceptable, in that this group receives the least benefit from taxes paid. For these reasons, although the real costs of an aging society might be less than those of a young society, doubts have been expressed about whether it is realistic or feasible to transfer previously private funds spent on children to the public domain for the benefit of the older population (Foot 1982, 135-136; Calvert 1977, 24-25; Stone and Fletcher 1980, 92-93; Stone and Marceau 1979, 81-83).

Part of the economic concern about demographic aging and appropriate policies stems from apprehension about a shift toward a public economy or a welfare state. That this issue is politically important was evident in the 1984 federal election in Canada, in which the Progressive Conservative Party, headed by Brian Mulroney, swept to power on a campaign platform of "less government involvement in the private sector." Concern about this issue is expressed in a different way by Herzog (1982, 128) when he refers to the "government-must-solve-it-myth." Private pension funds in Canada have grown to be the single largest source of private equity capital, as well as the major source of corporate borrowing (Myles 1984, 113). It becomes apparent that policy concerns about population aging are closely related to ideological issues of private versus public expenditures, as well as to issues of capital formation and consolidation. Power brokers who benefit from private pension schemes may resist increased public expenditure on the elderly. The policy issue thus becomes not one of a shifting demographic dependency burden but of vested economic interest. This was evident in the Canadian government initiative in 1985 and 1986 to differentially attract wealthy retirees as immigrants to Canada (Lipovenko 1985, 1).

It is likely, in the short run in Canada, that these complicated forces will result in a series of old-age security policies and programs that reflect the conflicts and contradictions out of which they grew. On one hand, there is the traditional Canadian concern for the less fortunate, the belief in entitlement to a decent pension after a lifetime of economic contribution, the unspoken agreement between generations to support the older group, and the growing political power of older people. On the other hand, there is resistance to expansion of the welfare state, concern about transferring private resources to the public sector, and concern about an investment empire being built on private pensions. All this no doubt means that future Canadian policies on pensions will be marked by compromise and "muddling through" to meet the immediate needs of Canadians. This, although not innovatively solving the economic problems of demographic aging, would be consistent with what Canada has done in the past (Myles 1984, 119).

Economic Problems of Older Women

Canada's aging population, as seen in Chapter 4, is one made up increasingly of women. The older a population is demographically, the greater the proportion of older women and widows in the population. Referred to by Stone and Fletcher (1980, 92) as an "ominous development," the sex imbalance in an aging population has profound economic policy implications. It has been argued that this development alone would tend to enlarge the role of governments in providing more security to the older population (Stone and Fletcher 1980, 92; Health and Welfare Canada 1982, 28-29), because fewer women than men have access to private pensions.

There are three essential components to the policy concerns about older women's economic security. The first is the question of eligibility for public and private pensions. The second is the more complicated problem of structural inequality, which places women in economically disadvantaged positions throughout their lives. The third is the issue of gender-based mortality tables, according to which women receive smaller pensions because they live longer.

With respect to eligibility for pensions, women face a number of obstacles, most of which are being debated by policy-makers at present (Health and Welfare Canada 1982, 28-29). Canada, unlike the United States and a few other industrialized countries, provides a universal flat-benefit pension to all Canadians as well as to others who meet Canadian residency requirements (Myles 1984, 60). Known as Old Age Security (OAS), this universal program came into effect in its present form in Canada in 1951 under the philosophy that individuals had a personal obligation to save for their old age (Weitz 1976, 136). OAS was amended in the early 1970s to provide an income-tested spouse's allowance for women aged 60-64 who did not yet qualify for OAS in their own right (Weitz 1975, 137). Since 1975, OAS has been indexed every three months to the consumer price index (Weitz 1976, 137). The Canadian federal government, in its spring 1985 budget, attempted to de-index these pensions, but this policy met with such protest from pensioners that the government was forced to withdraw the proposal. OAS is meant to provide a basic pension income to all citizens, regardless of labour force experience. It thus provides women who have spent their lives as homemakers a minimal pension income. OAS in 1985 is by no means a pension on which one can live, however, nor was it ever intended to be.

In addition to OAS, there are the Canada and Quebec Pension Plans, introduced in 1966 (Weitz 1975, 136) and the Guaranteed Income Supplement (GIS). The GIS provides a monthly income-tested pension supplement to pensioners who have no other source of income than OAS (Weitz 1975, 137). Given that women more often than men have had limited labour force experience, the GIS is more often of benefit to them. The Canada and Quebec Pension plans are mandatory wage-related pension schemes. All workers, whether employed or self-employed, contribute to the plans. Eligibility for benefits from these plans depends on years worked. In Canada, full benefits require forty years of work earnings (Myles 1984, 61), compared with thirty-nine years in the U.S. and thirty years in Sweden (Myles 1984, 61). Workers who have had intermittent work histories, limited earnings or no paid work experience at all are ineligible for full pensions. This, of course, affects women disproportionately.

Women have difficulty as well with the eligibility requirements of private pension plans. These often require a continuous minimal work history or a certain minimum level of earnings before one is eligible for benefits. Since women tend to have more interrupted work experience, and may work part-time or in jobs with low pay, they are often ineligible for private pension plans. Women, more often than men, work in jobs and situations with limited benefits packages. This means that some women with continuous labour force experience, such as domestics, day-care workers, and non-unionized factory workers, are excluded from private pension plans entirely.

Homemakers in Canada at present have no access to pensions in their own right, except for OAS (Health and Welfare Canada 1982, 29). This is an important policy issue at present in Canada. Many proponents of pensions for homemakers see as essential the provision of a pension income to women who have spent their lives caring for their homes and families (Canadian Advisory Council on the Status of Women, 1985). Opinion, however, is quite divided on how this could best be done. There is considerable agreement that opening Canada and Quebec Pension Plans to voluntary contributions from non-paid workers would be administratively difficult (Health and Welfare Canada 1982, 29). Improving survivors' benefits from other pensions has been suggested as a solution. A 1980 report on pensions (Statistics Canada 1982) reveals that about 30 percent of the members of public pension plans and approximately 78 percent of the members of private plans had no provision for pension benefits to go to the surviving spouse in the event of death.

The second component of the economic problems faced by older women relates closely to the first. Regardless of pension eligibility issues, men's and women's economic situations are quite different. A man and a woman, for example, on the brink of retirement often have unequal economic resources (Phillips and Phillips 1983). We have seen how women's different work histories limit their eligibility for pensions. It is also true that women earn considerably less than men do when they work. Women in Canada have been estimated to earn around 60 percent of what men earn (Wilson 1982, 106). Women have less job security, are much less likely to be in jobs that are unionized, and often have fewer benefits in the jobs they hold. This means that women often have fewer opportunities to save and plan for their retirement. They therefore have fewer options when they retire. This stems largely from the structured inequality by gender in our society.

Proposing to redress this inequality by pegging women's retirement income to that of their husbands', through improved survivor's benefits, is similar to seeing marriage as the societal solution to structured gender inequality. For a woman, marriage to a man who has better earning power than she has may be an economically rational solution to the problem of low earning power. This solution works, however, only as long as the marriage and the husband survive. On marital dissolution, women often face severe economic troubles (Wilson 1982, 20-21). The same is true when a husband dies, since pension benefits often die with him (Dulude 1984). It would be relatively straightforward to enact a policy of mandatory survivor's benefits. This was, in fact, recommended at the National Pensions Conference in 1982 (Health and Welfare Canada 1982, 29). However, women's problems of economic dependency in situations of marital dissolution are less easy to solve. The problem is compounded by women's considerably longer life expectancy. The ultimate solution would be for women to have access to their own pensions (Dulude 1981; Canadian Advisory Council on the Status of Women 1985).

The third component of the economic problems women face in an aging population seems, in light of the first two components, cruel in its application. This is the use of separate actuarial tables to compute men's and women's pension benefits. The issue here is not one of structured inequality, but differential treatment of women because of their longer life expectancy. Simply put, when a pension plan or an annuity comes due, some criteria must be used to decide how much of the total amount of money accumulated should be paid out each month. This requires an estimate of how long the pensioner is likely to live, so that the pension or annuity will not be used up before the person dies. The pension plan or insurance company needs to estimate, on a probabilistic basis, how long it will have to pay. Since women as a group live longer than men, pension plans quite correctly have calculated that they will have to pay benefits to women for a longer period of time. Thus, they argue, each monthly payment to women should be less than to men, to enable women pensioners to collect over a longer period. It has recently been argued that this is an example of discrimination against women. (It should be noted that in other realms, such as in health and life insurance, women are offered reduced rates for the same reason.) Critics of the use of two-sex tables have proposed that single-sex life tables be used to estimate pension or annuity payments. Several Supreme Court cases in the United States have prevented the use of sex-based actuarial tables to calculate pension benefits (OCUFA Forum 1985, 5). In Canada, this issue will likely be addressed soon by the legal system.

However the economic issues of women in an aging population are seen, the problems facing policy-makers today and in the future are real and pressing. As the Canadian population continues the aging process already begun a century ago, the economic plight of older women will become more of a problem. Steps are required immediately in both the public and private sectors to address the problems.

Economic Growth and Productivity

As we saw in Chapter 4, part of the concern and alarm about an aging population results from the fear that economic growth and productivity will diminish. We can divide the problem into three parts. The first is the issue of age-determined wages. The second is the contentious issue of mandatory retirement. The third, and related, issue is mobility.

Most people as they age tend to earn more. This is more true for men than for women because men have more continuous work experience and less substitutability. Women, by contrast, who return to the labour force after raising a family, or even after taking a year or two off to care for a baby, tend to go back to earnings that are the same or even below what they had when they left the labour force. There is, however, a clear pattern for workers in most occupations to command higher salaries as they age. This becomes an issue in an aging society because the work force is increasingly composed of people who command high salaries. Pressure is placed, therefore, on older workers to increase their productivity to justify their higher salaries. If a large segment of the work force is composed of older workers, it may appear as if productivity is declining as salaries increase. Employers seem to be paying out more of their profits in salaries. This is the issue of age-related wages in an aging society.

There are related policy concerns in both private and public sectors. In the public sector, the government of Canada has recently attempted to solve the productivity "problem" in the aging federal civil service by providing special bonuses to those who elect early retirement. This option was made available to many top-management federal civil servants in 1985. In a broader public policy sense, incentives have been provided by both provincial and federal governments to increase productivity, often by cutting taxes paid by corporations. The principle here is to give industry a "boost" of vitality, thereby enhancing worker productivity in the newly dynamic companies. Other such attempts can be expected in the future.

In the private sector, the problem of an aging work force has been addressed, in part, by terminating aging executives and workers before they become eligible for pensions. This procedure is likely to be seriously challenged under Canada's new Charter of Rights, as a form of age discrimination. Another approach, which has been used for many years, is a differential benefits package for younger workers. People joining a company in their youth actually build up equity in pensions, insurance and other benefits. Older workers, unless they started with the company as young people, do not usually have as many benefits. This may be an attempt at undercutting the total wages or salaries commanded by older employees.

The second policy issue concerning economic growth and productivity in an aging society is the very controversial one of mandatory retirement. The question of mandatory retirement relates to economic productivity and growth in two ways. The first is that mandatory retirement is regarded by some analysts as a mechanism for easing out older workers (who are paid top wages) without having to make a case for incompetence or diminished productivity (*Globe and Mail* editorial, 29 July 1985). The second is that mandatory retirement presumably makes way for younger workers with new ideas to join the work force.

Recently in Canada, mandatory retirement at age 65 has been challenged under the Charter of Rights by the Canadian Association of University Teachers as age discrimination (*Globe and Mail* 29 July 1985). Ten doctors at a British Columbia hospital have been successful, at least temporarily, in the British Columbia Supreme Court in having their admitting privileges restored, despite the fact that they are over the age of 65 (*Globe and Mail* 2 August 1985). The legal issue here seems to be civil rights under the Charter versus productivity of corporations and social institutions. It could be argued that mandatory retirement is not a violation of civil rights, just as not permitting people under 21 to vote is not a violation of rights. A crucial aspect of this important debate, however, is the issue of productivity and competence in an aging society. It is feared that as the Canadian population ages, productivity will decline, as the salaries of an aging work force continue to rise. (It should be kept in mind that productivity is a relationship between output (work done) and input (wages), so that if one worker is paid more than another for essentially the same work, he/she is the less productive worker.) Whether this fear is well based in fact or not is almost irrelevant. The most productive and vibrant organizations are those that experience a regular influx of "fresh blood" by way of new young recruits and have a work force that is age-varied. Abolishing mandatory retirement could interfere with societal productivity, not because the older workers are less productive as individuals, but simply because they are the most highly paid and will constitute a larger proportion of the work force.

Abolishing mandatory retirement could also affect productivity and economic growth in the area of mobility. An older worker who obtains the right to continue in his/her highly paid position may block the hiring and advancement of younger workers. Given the typical cost of one senior level position in universities for example, keeping on a senior professor beyond retirement age blocks the hiring of approximately three junior professors. This thwarting of young people in their search for work cannot help but be disenchanting. In the 1980s in Canada, this experience is all too common for many young university graduates. Abolishing mandatory retirement would diminish the hopes of youth even further, with consequent effects on their productivity, not only while they are looking for work but possibly throughout their lifetimes.

Policy issues surrounding economic growth and productivity are very complex indeed. Enactment of a policy that might seem equitable for one group may have serious negative connotations for another or for society at large. Considerable care and thought must precede policy changes in this arena.

RETIREMENT AND WORK ISSUES

A number of policy issues in the area of retirement and work are raised by Canada's aging population. Since work forms a good part of the identity of most Canadians and defines much of what they do with their lives, understanding changing issues surrounding work in an aging society is fundamental to understanding population aging. That these issues receive less public attention than economic issues does not make them less important. In many ways, policy decisions on work and retirement may be closer to the hearts of Canadians than economic policy decisions, which primarily touch their purses. In this chapter, three areas are discussed: the growing number of retirees, the changing meaning of work, and the policy implications of volunteer contributions. (Individual-level issues involved in retirement and work go beyond the scope of this book and will be addressed in subsequent publications in the Aging Series.)

The Growing Number of Retirees

The experience of retirement from paid work will be more common in the future as the population ages. A peak in retirements will occur in Canada in the 2020s and 2030s, at which time most of the baby boom generation will be retired or retiring. The meaning of retirement differs from individual to individual, depending on work commitment and orientation to leisure, but retirement is also a social phenomenon. The time at which retirement occurs is socially determined. Retirement has implications that are both social and economic, and it is these implications that most policy issues address.

As more and more people number among the retired, the meaning of retirement will change. Some of the issues in financing retirement, most of which involve policy changes or adjustments, have already been discussed. The experience of retirement will become more diversified as more people experience it. Research now indicates that, although retirement is a major transition, most people successfully adjust and experience relatively little stress (McPherson 1983, 367-368; Foner and Schwab 1983, 72; MacLean 1983). This counters the widespread belief that retirement is often a stressful experience. Nonetheless, retirement for a minority of people is unwelcome, either because they are forced to accept compulsory retirement or because they are unprepared to make the transition from paid work to increased leisure.

As the numbers of retired people increase, the numbers of people facing retirement unwillingly also increase. Although people who feel this way will not likely be a majority, programs in the future might be implemented to ease the transition. The alternative is for retirement policies to change so that retirement age becomes more flexible. Those who wish to stay on could, perhaps at reduced load and reduced salary. This idea has been implemented recently by a number of Canadian universities. It is one innovative approach to the problems of productivity and blocked mobility channels for younger workers that occur when older people are kept on at full salary after the retirement age.

Among the increased numbers of retirees in future, many more might choose early retirement. This would be consistent with the research evidence that shows that many people would retire earlier if they could afford to do so (McPherson 1983, 368). As attitudes toward work and leisure change (to be discussed in more detail in the next section of this chapter), and as more companies provide incentives to older workers to retire early, retirement at 55 or 60 or even earlier might become more popular. The policy challenge here is that pension funds might be overtaxed. This would be particularly problematic if large numbers of the baby boom generation took early retirement at the same time. In planning policies for an aging Canadian society, these possibilities must be projected and anticipated.

Given the increased female labour force participation in Canada over the past few decades, and the differential life expectancy of women, many retirees in the future will be women. In view of the traditional patterns of age at marriage and women's increasing commitment to lifetime employment, policy-makers in the future may have to think in terms of a couple's retirement plans, rather than only in terms of an individual's retirement. If a married woman chooses to continue working after her husband's retirement, there may be implications for his pension. If she chooses to retire early, the traditional pattern in the past, adjustments may be made in her pension. Policy-makers might be well advised to estimate costs and savings involved in these various options. An attempt might also be made to implement policies that would not provoke increased marital disharmony through problems created by pension schemes.

Although much less is known about women's retirement experiences than about men's (McPherson 1983, 389), there is little doubt that women's experiences in the future will become more important. More women will be in the retirement ages than ever before. More women in the future will also experience lifelong work. Research on women's retirement is sparse and contradictory (McPherson 1983, 340). Some studies have found few sex differences in retirement attitudes and adjustments. Others have found that women retirees are less satisfied than men. Given women's average pension and annuity prospects, this is not entirely surprising. A larger proportion of older women than older men live out their last years in poverty and poor health (McPherson 1983, 390). Women, unlike men, tend to become more politically active with age. As more women face retirement with inadequate pensions, we could see the emergence of women pensioners' rights groups or lobby groups patterned on the "Grey Panthers" in the United States (McPherson 1983, 31). The entire question of women's retirement prospects needs to be examined carefully, and appropriate policy decisions taken in the immediate future.

The Changing Meaning of Work

Work provides a lifestyle, a circle of friends, an identity, and defines a major portion of most people's lives. Whether work is intrinsically valued or done to pay the rent, attitudes toward it are important in defining retirement and old age. Work may be taking on a different meaning in Canada today, and this change may have important policy implications.

There are several cross-cutting trends in the changing meaning of work in Canada. All have implications for future policies in an aging society. There is the intensified search for meaningful work. Some people in North America are no longer satisfied to work hard, pay off the mortgage and get regular promotions. They search for intrinsic rewards in the work they do. This search has led to an increasing number of midlife career changes among people in middle- or upper-class occupations (McPherson 1983, 373). In the future, retirement may not be a once-in-a-lifetime experience, nor the transition from paid work to leisure. Retirement could occur several times within a lifetime, as career changes are made. The significance of retirement may change dramatically from what it was when a person had a single career, often a single job, from which he/she retired. Given that an increasing number of future retirees come from the idealistic baby boom generation, we can expect more multiple retirements in the future in Canada.

Young Canadians are also in search of meaningful work. Unlike their elders, many seem more interested in job satisfaction than in high pay, mobility or job security. This requirement, when compounded by the chronic unemployment faced by many Canadian young people today, may give younger workers limited opportunity to contribute consistently to a pension plan. They also could have rather different attitudes toward retirement than their elders. Some might postpone retirement until they are eligible for a good pension. Others could welcome retirement as an opportunity to pursue meaningful leisure activities, to contribute to society through volunteer work, or to start a business. Whatever happens, these changes deserve careful attention by policy-makers.

Another changed work pattern may be the more intermittent work lives of men. Women have always tended to have interrupted careers. As men become more involved in the raising of children, in housework and family life generally, they too might have less consistent work patterns. There is some indication that working-class men who are less able to find work or are laid off from their jobs may choose to work at home, while their wives, who are less often unionized and more poorly paid, may continue to have jobs. This may mean that men's and women's work patterns, in some occupations, will become more similar. Policy questions are raised about the structure of pension schemes that now are premised largely on a male breadwinner.

Women's increased commitment to full-time, lifelong work is another trend in Canada. There have always been women in Canada who had careers and a similar attitude toward work as men. Recently, however, the numbers and proportions of such women have increased. This is true not only for women in the professions or in high-level positions, whose numbers have not grown that much over the past 50 years or so, but for women in a variety of occupations (Wilson 1982). The retirement needs for lifelong working women are different than for women who have worked at home or for women with an interrupted work life. Pension schemes for women are still not at the level they are for men. The assumption still seems to be that women, no matter what their work commitment or experiences, are men's dependants. It is assumed that their husbands' pension plans will provide for them (although the husband may be nonexistent because of divorce, separation, or death, or because the woman never married). Further, myths and misconceptions about women's family roles have prevented the development of pension and insurance schemes that protect the woman's dependants. These are crucial policy issues in a society that will be increasingly composed of women in an aging Canada.

Policy Implications of Volunteer Work

Canadians see work as something one is paid to do. It has been shown, however, that much work is done without pay. Women's unpaid work at home is a classic example of volunteer work. Men's handiwork around the house would be another example, as would service work in a variety of organizations. Work may be defined as something done for the good of society, whether paid or unpaid. It seems that voluntary, unpaid work is vital to the Canadian economy.

Retirement is often seen as a time to stop work and begin leisure. In the future, policy changes and incentives might unite meaningful work with the desire to contribute voluntarily. If a person facing mandatory retirement, for example, wishes to continue to work, he/she might be able to continue that work as a volunteer or on his/her own without compensation or for reduced compensation. This would not work well in all fields; however, in some fields it is an excellent solution to the problem posed by older productive workers who wish to continue working but not to collect the same high salaries. We are not talking here necessarily about the traditional volunteer position, the hospital "grey lady" or "meals on wheels" volunteers. Volunteer work could be done in business or professional settings. Teachers, for example, might aid in curriculum development, counselling students, advising young teachers, etc. University professors might continue to do research or teach a class but no longer undertake administrative duties. This blurring of the distinction between work and leisure could be a healthy step. It would require policy changes to ensure that retired people's pensions would not be affected. Enormous benefit to society could be gained as older people continue to contribute actively, but do not create resentment among younger workers by continuing to draw pay at their previous levels.

HEALTH ISSUES

The area of health, particularly rising health care costs, is a major concern, in view of Canada's aging population. Older people are thought to be more often in need of health care, particularly chronic care. In a population composed of more older people, health care costs, like the costs of pensions, are anticipated to increase dramatically.

Policy issues in provision of health care in an aging society are complex and multifaceted. To understand these issues really requires a full understanding of the problems of the Canadian health care system in the 1980s. This is beyond the scope of a book on demographic aging. However, in this section, many of the policy issues facing the health care system in Canada in the future will be discussed as issues arising from an aging society. It is not because an aging society creates the problems, but that it places pressure on the health care system in such a way as to emphasize its weak points. Five areas of health policy concerning Canada's aging population will be considered here: the health care system in Canada, myths and misconceptions about aging and health care provision in an aging Canada, aging and health care costs, and policy issues relating to the ideal quality of life.

General Policy Concerns of Health Care in Canada

Many of the health policy issues raised by the acceleration of population aging are not problems of an aging society but problems of the health care system itself, which are exacerbated by population aging.

People's health depends on many factors other than the absence of illness, disease or disability. Income security, housing conditions, stress, workplace safety, family structure, social contacts, leisure activities, happiness with one's situation, smoking, drinking and risk-taking while driving all affect one's health. Despite evidence that these factors matter, the health care system in Canada is premised, to a large degree, on the medical model (Lalonde 1978), which sees illness as the result of the body's malfunctioning. The solution to bodily malfunctioning is biochemical or surgical intervention. This approach is often costly, highly interventionist and sometimes inappropriate to the problem.

Canada's system of health care has been called a health cure system because of its reliance on the medical model of cure (Lalonde 1978). Health care, in fact, might involve non-medical approaches such as lifestyle counselling, stress management, exercise programs or nutrition advice. It might also involve improving the workplace, solving family problems, and providing better housing, a more adequate income or more leisure time options. Seldom are these part of the health care system in Canada, as it is presently structured. In fact, it could be argued that disincentives to meet these needs are built into the health care system. A doctor, for example, who takes the time to counsel a patient on nutrition or on coping with life's problems will not be rewarded nearly as highly as one who writes a prescription or performs a medical procedure or test. This is because most provincial health insurance schemes provide fees for service, regardless of how long the doctor spent with the patient.

Canada's cure system, based on the medical model, is aimed largely at those who have acute illnesses or accidents, for which medical intervention is most helpful. These types of problems are amenable to immediate cure. Doctors, nurses and hospitals are well rewarded because they can save the life of an accident victim or cure a life-threatening illness. Public health nurses who give vaccinations to isolated native children are accorded less prestige. Even lower in terms of prestige are those who provide counselling on fitness, diet, stress or coping. As a result, patients with medical problems that are most amenable to cure tend to receive the most attention.

This focus on cure makes the Canadian health care system less open to *prevention* of illness, disease or disability. The basic premise is that problems will be treated as they occur. The notion of preventing problems in the first place is seen to lie in other realms than medicine. This does not mean that the health care system is averse to prevention, but that it simply lacks the resources to prevent illness. Major exceptions, of course, are the areas of public health, occupational health and to some extent dentistry, in which good preventive medicine is practised.

One of the challenges facing the Canadian health care system is to build rewards for counselling into the system of payments by provincial health insurance schemes. Building prevention into the system is another policy concern at present. Policy-makers are examining the degree to which government funding could go to meet contemporary needs for chronic care or home care, as opposed to the more expensive acute care in the hospital. As Canadian society ages, there is little doubt that these challenges will become more pressing.

Myths and Misconceptions about Aging and Health

There is no question that Canada's older population at present has higher rates of hospital utilization than the younger population (Stone and Fletcher 1980, 45). During the 1970s this utilization by older people increased relative to utilization by the total population. Women at younger ages are hospitalized more than men, but older men are hospitalized much more often than older women (Stone and Fletcher 1980, 45). Diseases of the circulatory system, cancer, mental problems and musculoskeletal diseases number prominently among problems for which older people are hospitalized (Stone and Fletcher 1980, 44).

The older population as a whole, however, is remarkably healthy and remains functionally well until very advanced ages (Health and Welfare Canada 1982, 43). Approximately 80 percent of people over the age of 65 in Canada are capable of living independently and caring for themselves (Health and Welfare Canada 1982, 43). This is in spite of the fact that 75 percent of older people suffer from at least one chronic health problem, ranging from arthritis to heart conditions (Health and Welfare Canada 1982, 43). The Canada Health Survey of 1978–79 found that 46 percent of people 65 years and older either never visited a doctor or made fewer than two visits during the year prior to the survey. This compares with 66 percent of those under the age of 65 (Health and Welfare Canada 1982, 44). Another measure of the health status of older people is the inverse measure of mortality. Canada, like most Western countries, has experienced a sharp decline in mortality levels among the elderly population in the past 10–15 years, indicating that older people are probably healthier than they used to be.

No illnesses, diseases or disabilities are unique to older people. Many illnesses, however, such as arthritis, mental problems, heart problems and cancer, occur more often among older people. Senility is now recognized as a "wastebasket diagnosis" for mental illnesses suffered by the old (Health and Welfare Canada 1982, 45). Most mental disorders occurring in the elderly result from depression and other non-organic causes, rather than from deterioration of bodies and brains as a result of aging (Health and Welfare Canada 1982, 45). Considerable controversy exists about mental deterioration among the elderly, with many critics attributing it to misdiagnosis or lack of concern by the medical establishment in tracking down the real problem.

Another misconception is that most, or many, older people require institutionalization in a chronic care facility or a nursing home. A precise estimate of how many older people are receiving long-term care is difficult because of the definitional problem of what constitutes long-term care. A "collective dwelling," for example, could be a retirement building in which no one receives any kind of health care on the premises, or it could be a nursing home with intensive medical care. Estimates of the institutional health care provided to the elderly in Canada in the early 1980s range from under 6 percent to just over 10 percent (Health and Welfare Canada 1982, 46). This is far from a majority of older persons. If present trends toward home care and community services continue, this percentage could decline considerably.

The prevalence of health problems among the elderly in Canada rose by one-half in the period between the Canada Sickness Survey in 1950–51 and the Canada Health Survey of 1978–79 (Health and Welfare Canada 1982, 47). This was a period during which the older population doubled in size. The prevalence of long-term disability among older people remained constant over the 30-year period. Older Canadians are becoming healthier, living longer, adjusting to their chronic illnesses better and finding new approaches to any long-term care needs that arise. No clear one-to-one relationship emerges between growth in the older population and dramatic increases in health care costs (Siegel and Hoover 1982).

Health Care Provision

Although an aging population need not mean a dramatic escalation in demand for long-term care or hospitalization, the care requirements of an aging society may differ somewhat from those of a more youthful society. In addition, the health care needs of the elderly of today may differ substantially from those of the elderly in the future. The Canadian health care system, too, is changing, and might look rather different in the next decades. Planning for the health needs of an aging society is not a straightforward process. Much of what follows is necessarily speculative.

The issue of costs has received most of the attention, in discussion of health care policies for an aging society. Less attention has been given to the changing health needs of an aging society. Lack of knowledge in this regard is compounded by the cure orientation of the Canadian health care system, and by the commonly held belief that individual aging is a less than natural process. The consequence may be that older Canadians overutilize the health care system (Bayne and Wigdor 1980, Part 4). It is not because they are irresponsible or self-indulgent, but because of the structure and biases in the provision of health care.

Two examples might illustrate this. An older woman complains to her doctor of arthritic pain. Rather than attributing it to aging and prescribing a pain-killer, the doctor may intervene surgically in the hope of curing the problem. Thus, acute care facilities are used inefficiently. It is not that the doctor is incompetent (although some might argue otherwise) but rather that the pressures of the system encourage him/her to intervene, even in situations in which intervention may not help. Our second example deals with a rather common situation. An older person who is relatively healthy becomes forgetful and depressed. Because of the shortage of home care and community services, this person is hospitalized or placed in a chronic care facility. Intensive care is thus provided to a person who does not require it, thereby overutilizing and misusing health care facilities. Had adequate community services been available, costs could have been reduced and care appropriate to the situation could have been provided. If the elderly are overusing the health care system in Canada at present, it may be due to a lack of other options.

Projecting this overuse into the future, without allowing for changes in the health care system or the improvement of special services for the elderly, may result in an overestimate of future health care utilization. A further difficulty with projecting present trends is that prevention of illness and disability are not considered. Indications are that, in the future, more attention will be devoted to preventive medicine, to lifestyle changes and social changes that will simultaneously postpone illness and disability among older people and dispel ageism. As pointed out by Riley and Bond (1983, 243–52), the problem requires a multifronted approach: research to dispel myths that disabilities are inevitable with advancing age, policy and attitudinal changes that would involve older people more actively in society, and changes in health care delivery so that the elderly are not "overtreated." Riley and Bond (1983) aptly illustrate how stereotypes and policy interact to make society, health care workers, and the elderly themselves see old people as more ill than they actually are.

What changes may be needed in Canada's health care system in anticipation of the growing numbers of older people? Some researchers such as Stone and MacLean (cited in Stone and Fletcher 1980, 47) see the aging Canadian population as requiring a substantial increase in hospital services, with a small increase in physician services. Others (Health and Welfare Canada 1982, 59) see less need for expanded hospital services, provided that there are other policy changes in health care. Among these are an increased emphasis on health promotion, so as to postpone the onset of disabling illness and enhance the probability that the elderly can live longer independently. Fitness and mental health programs for the middle-aged and elderly (Health and Welfare Canada 1982, 55) could add years of healthy autonomy to the lives of older people.

Better coordination and integration of social and health services becomes more necessary in an aging population where people's health needs are often linked to socio-economic problems (Health and Welfare Canada 1982, 56–57; Connidis 1985). Educating health care workers about the deleterious effects of ageism is also essential. Providing for the cost of eyeglasses, hearing aids and other medical devices could cut the cost of acute long-term care for the elderly (Health and Welfare Canada 1982, 58). The development of hospices outside hospitals to care humanely for the dying would be beneficial as well as cost-saving. Greater reliance on community and home support services could reduce the need for institutional care for the very old (Health and Welfare Canada 1982, 59). Planning for the adequate provision of health services in an aging population is not easy, but it is a challenge that we should welcome with innovative ideas.

Health Care Costs

The issue of increasing health care costs in an aging population evokes almost as much alarm as the issue of pensions. This is not surprising, since analysts who forecast future pension and health costs tend to project forward what we are experiencing now. However, an aging population may create entirely new demands on the health care system, not merely increased demands for the same kind of expensive medical care we have been receiving.

At least two simulation studies have been undertaken in Canada on the demographic pressures placed on health care by an aging society. The study done by Stone and MacLean in 1978 (cited by Stone and Fletcher 1980, 46–47) focussed on physician-service usage in Saskatchewan. They found that even though the numbers of patients seen by physicians did not increase much with population aging, the costs increased rather dramatically. Population aging alone tends to add $3 per capita to medical care costs

(Stone and Fletcher 1980, 46). A steeper rise in hospital costs over time is predicted, even without greatly increased utilization. Stone and Fletcher (1980,47) conclude that "cost pressures related to health service delivery will be important factors in the overall change that senior citizens will make upon the future gross national product."

Another simulation (Denton and Spencer 1982b) also estimates the degree to which population aging increases health care costs in Canada. Regardless of the projection assumptions used, expenditures on health care increase substantially in the future. By 2026, for example, health care is projected to require an additional 1.5 to 2 percent of the Canadian gross national product (Denton and Spencer 1982b, 10). These researchers suggest that such increases in the costs of health care could possibly be offset by technological advances or by resource-saving policy changes in health care delivery. For example, the large-scale use of nurse-practitioners in addition to doctors could save about 7 percent (Denton and Spencer 1982b, 12).

It is not clear how much the aging Canadian population will increase health care costs. Costs, however, will rise. Whether they will increase to the extent predicted by the simulations remains uncertain. To a large degree, this depends on what changes are made in society and in the health care system to improve the health and quality of life of old people. Improvements could offset the health care cost increases of an aging society. Innovations in health care delivery are needed. "It is certain, however, that the provision of health and social services to the aged will not contribute to national productivity and economic wealth. Instead, their provision should be seen as the mark of a civilized society" (Health and Welfare Canada 1982, 47).

Quality of Life

It is widely believed that advancing age is necessarily associated with decreased quality of life, either through biological or mental deterioration or through diminished socio-economic status. The interaction of economic status and assumed physical deterioration is important to quality of life issues. Ill health or the onset of disability is not randomly distributed in society or among the aged. As Wilkins (1983, 2) suggests, "... the burden of ill health in Canada continues to fall disproportionately on the most disadvantaged segments of the population." Disability-free life expectancy in Canada is, on average, 7.7 years longer for the rich than for the poor (Wilkins 1983, 14). Some gerontologists call this phenomenon "multiple jeopardy": older members of discriminated-against minorities often suffer in old age to a greater extent than others. In fact, a lower quality of life is experienced throughout the lives of the disadvantaged, and this situation is exacerbated by the onset of old age.

Recognition that old age may mean a significant deterioration in quality of life and actual length of life for disadvantaged groups enables policy-makers to target these groups for special consideration. The issue of quality of life goes beyond mere access to health care. The needs for income security and a decent standard of living seem paramount.

Data show (Wilkins 1983) that even with state-subsidized universal health care, life expectancies differ across classes. The upper class experiences a much higher quality of life in old age than other classes. Members of the upper class are more often married, have wider social networks, better housing, better food, more leisure, better health, greater respect from the community and greater mobility (McPherson 1983, 258). Furthermore, they hold fewer negative attitudes about aging (McPherson 1983, 258) and are subjected to fewer stereotypes. This suggests that quality of life issues are, at root, issues of class, inequality and income. The old do not universally suffer from a decline in quality of life. The poor, however, suffer a large decline, evidenced by their much higher mortality rates. A long step toward improving quality of life could be taken by improving the economic situations of older people.

A second policy issue concerning quality of life is the age of onset of disability. Wilkins (1983, 12) calculates what he calls "quality-adjusted life expectancy," or that portion of life expectancy that is free from restriction, from long-term disability or institutionalization. Wilkins finds that people with limited incomes have more disabilities and require more institutionalization and long-term care. They do not live as long as people with more economic resources, and in addition they spend a greater proportion of their later years in pain. This increases the public costs of health care and limits the contribution made by these people to society.

Another quality of life issue is raised by people concerned about life-prolonging medical technology. Older people in Canada do not often die a natural death. With modern medical technology, it is possible to die several deaths — a death of the lifestyle that you lived most of your life, a death of consciousness, a heart death or a brain death. It is possible, and even likely, unless the patient makes his/her wishes known in advance, that a person who is dead in most respects will be kept alive by artificial means. Policy questions are raised about who decides, when, and how, and what the implications of such decisions are.

HOUSING AND FAMILY ISSUES

The home and housing are often neglected as policy issues related to Canada's aging population. Yet they are vitally important, if somewhat less complex and diverse than issues affecting health care. Our discussion here concerns the changing family in Canadian society, and housing and home care for the elderly.

The Changing Canadian Family

Canadian society is experiencing an acceleration in demographic aging as a result of changes in the family, most notably declining fertility, as seen in Chapter 3. Canadian families have become dramatically smaller over the past two or so decades. This decline in family size, combined with the increasing cost of home heating in a country with a climate as inhospitable as Canada's, has meant that families are living in smaller accommodations. Related to the decline in family size is the increased work force participation of women, particularly married women with children.

Other changes include the decline in multigeneration living arrangements, as more and more people choose to live apart from their families (Connidis and Rempel 1983). Children are choosing to live apart from their parents (although the early 1980s saw an increase in adult children living at home or returning home out of economic necessity). Older parents seem to prefer independence to living with their adult children. Some ethnic groups provide an exception to this rule, however (Health and Welfare Canada 1982, 84). With increased mobility, modern families are likely to live far away from their older parents and siblings.

Another recent change in Canadian families is the increased longevity and health of older people. Middle-aged Canadian couples sometimes have as many as two sets of parents and perhaps even grandparents, all of whom are retired. Even if the families do not actually share a household, the emotional, social and financial demands of such families can be enormous.

The increased rate of divorce and separation has consequences in an aging population. Adult children might not have the financial resources to assist an older parent, if they are supporting children of their own. Divorced adult children may lack the requisite emotional stability and security to enable them to cope with the needs of an aging parent. They may be living in common-law relationships that could pose problems for the aging parent. The increasing divorce rate has also meant that aging parents are more often alone, sometimes after a lifetime of being married. Parents who are divorced may feel lost, resourceless and more dependent on their adult children than they might otherwise be. More single and divorced elderly people are institutionalized than are people who remain married late in life (Health and Welfare Canada 1982, 79). The problem of divorce affects older women more than men because women are less likely to remarry. Women also live longer, on average, than their ex-mates and often have fewer financial resources than older men have.

Differential life expectancy between men and women also means that older women are more likely to be left alone as widows. Widows make up a considerable portion of the over 65 age group (over half in 1976), while widowers make up approximately 20 percent of this age group (Health and Welfare Canada 1982, 80; Northcott 1984). The number of widows in the older Canadian population is expected to grow by 36 percent between 1975 and 2000. Among women over the age of 75, during this period, the proportion widowed is expected to grow by 100 percent (Health and Welfare Canada 1982, 80). Given limited pension provisions for widows, these women are often without adequate income.

All these changes in Canadian families make the family less able to cope with the needs of aging parents. Families are often far away, living in small apartments or houses, divorced, unsettled financially, or forced to cope with several aging relatives at once, as well as children who are still at home. In addition, the needs of aging parents, particularly those of women, are increasing since they are more often alone and without adequate financial resources. These changes underline the need for changed attitudes and policies about care for the elderly. It is not the case, as is commonly thought, that children are uncaring about the plight of their parents, or grandchildren about their grandparents. The realities of the Canadian family are such that recent changes make it difficult to appropriately respond to the needs of elderly family members. It is no longer easy for grown children, no matter how well-meaning, to accommodate their elderly parents. Policies in contemporary Canada have failed to reflect this new reality and implicitly tend to blame people for not caring adequately for their aging parents.

Housing and Home Care

Data on the housing needs of the older population are in remarkably short supply in Canada, but there seems to be a large unmet need (Stone and Fletcher 1980, 49). Predictions indicate that the housing needs of older people will put considerable strain on the pensions these people receive, unless housing policies for the elderly are adjusted.

Most elderly people in Canada own their own homes (Health and Welfare Canada 1982, 61). Although this may seem to provide autonomy and independence, it should be noted that many of the homes in which older people live are also older, requiring substantial unkeep as well as high heating costs. The one-third of older people who live in apartments have newer accommodation and smaller quarters (Health and Welfare Canada 1982, 62). Apartments that are affordable to the elderly, many of whom are widows, are often subsidized and age-segregated. These apartments are often located in places with poor accessibility to shopping and services (Gutman 1980, 198-99). If the present-day shortage of acceptable and affordable housing for older people continues, Gutman (1980, 200) worries that more older people will continue to stay in their homes. This, she feels, could increase the cost of home care, not only because of the increased number of older persons continuing to live in their own homes, but also because older people in their own homes will be even older and frailer.

An important question is whether the provision of high quality, comfortable, accessible and affordable retirement housing can serve to prevent the onset of disability and dependency (Gutman 1980, 200). Good housing may, if well planned, enable older people to retain their autonomy and freedom, without having the heavy responsibilities of home upkeep or the fear of being alone. Research clearly is needed on the types of retirement housing that would be welcomed by older people. Policies must be established to benefit the homeowner who sells to move into retirement housing; if the older person selling his/her home will suffer an economic loss, no matter how attractive the option of retirement housing is, older people will continue to live in their own homes.

Older people are among the primary recipients of housing assistance from the federal and provincial governments in Canada (Health and Welfare Canada 1982, 63). Loans are provided, at reduced rates, to construct senior citizens' housing of various types. As well, subsidies are available to reduce rents in housing for older people with low incomes. Despite these efforts, there are long waiting lists of older people in many places in Canada for good housing at subsidized rates (Stone and Fletcher 1980, 49). This housing shortage underlines the close relationship between the social needs of older people and their economic plight. If more older persons had decent pensions, the problems of housing would be less severe. As the numbers of older people grow in Canadian society, the problem of finding affordable, acceptable housing will worsen.

Planning for the future aging of the Canadian population is obviously essential, and innovative programs are required. A number of ideas are being tried on an experimental basis now. For example, "granny flats" (an inappropriate, i.e. gender-biased, label for an interesting idea) have been introduced recently in southern Ontario. These are self-contained small houses, which are installed on relatives' property. The arrangement, borrowed from Australia, gives older people the independence of their own accommodation close to relatives. An inexpensive alternative to senior citizens' housing, it may work well for many families. Another innovative alternative might be cooperative housing in which unrelated older people share accommodation. For some, this would be a violation of privacy. For others, it might provide the companionship they need to continue to live an independent life. Other ideas might include the establishment of cottage communities, mobile home parks or condominium units, especially for older people. These have worked successfully in other parts of the world, most notably in the southern and southwestern United States. Some urban alternatives include the development of apartment hotels or high-rise condominiums.

Older people who wish to stay in their own homes could possibly take on reverse mortgages. Popular in Europe, these mortgages enable elderly homeowners to borrow money on the equity they have in their homes. Payments made by the lender to the homeowner are generally not considered income, but a loan (Health and Welfare Canada 1982, 71). Older homeowners might benefit from subsidized assistance to convert their homes into apartments. The availability of a greater number of options for housing would benefit many older people.

There is evidence to indicate that the longer an older person is kept in the family or in the community, the longer the onset of disability can be avoided or postponed (Gutman 1980). Given the changing patterns of family life in Canada today, this is not easily arranged. A major impediment is the lack of family members to look after the older person during the day. The person may not require much care, perhaps only the preparation of a lunch or the administering of medicine. Present policies for the elderly make home services difficult to obtain. Sometimes families make the difficult choice of institutionalizing an older parent because they cannot find adequate services to meet their minimal needs at home. More flexibility in housing policies for the elderly is necessary. It is clear that Canadian families and the needs of older people have changed and will continue to change.

EDUCATION ISSUES

In discussions of shifting educational policy in an aging society, it is sometimes mistakenly assumed that the problem is simple. As the population ages, the argument goes, fewer resources are required for the education of young people and more for pensions and health care for older people. This shift in expenditures will indeed be necessary but, as we have seen, it is not as simple a process as some would have us believe.

There has been a lack of attention, in the past at least, to the demographic bases of educational enrolments in Canada (Foot 1982, 145). Since school attendance is compulsory for children between the ages of six and fifteen in most provinces, enrolments mirror the rises and falls in the birth rate and, to a lesser extent, the rates of immigration and interprovincial migration. Educational planners have a period of at least five years (since school entry of a cohort occurs five to six years after birth) in which to plan how many classrooms, teachers, librarians and books are needed in the future. The increasing numbers of vacant public schools in Canada in the 1980s testify to a lack of educational planning. It has been suggested that these unused schools be transformed into retirement housing. This would be a direct transfer from the young to the old, from expenditure on youth to expenditure on the old.

In Canada in the mid-1980s, there are considerably fewer school-age children than there have been in the past. (The one exception to this is that the number of preschoolers has been rising since 1976 (Statistics Canada 1984a, 37). This is not because the birth rate has gone up, but because mothers in the large baby boom generation are now having children.) Declining enrolments in schools are a consequence of the aging Canadian population. This situation will soon affect universities as well.

Educational policy is thus an area that can be considerably influenced by demographic age structure shifts. The challenge of educational planning becomes greater in an aging society. Population projections are useful, but sound analyses of the future of fertility and migration trends are essential, as is understanding of the importance of shifting generation size. Of particular significance is the degree to which the birth rate is likely to remain constant. Fluxes and flows in the birth rate play havoc with educational planning.

Most of the educational funds that will be transferred to meet the needs of the elderly are expected to come from elementary and secondary school coffers. This is because declines in enrolment as a result of the declining birth rate are most pronounced at the younger ages. Older people are also less likely to make use of elementary and secondary education. However, they do attend postsecondary schools and no doubt will do so in increasing numbers in the future. However, policy-makers in Canada do not see, at present, increasing demand by returning students as a solution to cutbacks in postsecondary education (Foot 1982, 182).

Educational policy issues in an aging society go well beyond young-to-old transfers, however. Many older people, often for the first time, have leisure time. For increasing numbers, this freedom allows the opportunity for education (Health and Welfare Canada 1982, 114). Education can take the form of a non-credit, general interest class. It can also take the form of working toward a higher degree at a community college or university. Many Canadian colleges and universities now regularly offer courses and programs at reduced tuition to retirees. There are also summer residential learning experiences or "ElderHostels" for older people at some universities (Health and Welfare Canada 1982, 115). Many provincial governments, which have primary responsibility for education in Canada, underwrite the costs of these programs. Correspondence courses or courses offered on television are also popular with older people in Canada. Libraries are increasingly stocking big-print books and book tapes for older students. In some provinces, such as Saskatchewan, programs are sponsored by the provincial government to educate older people on aging so they can assist, advise and counsel other older people (Health and Welfare Canada 1982, 116).

Current participation of the elderly in higher education is not extensive. Universities still focus largely on educating the young (Health and Welfare Canada 1982, 117). Certain impediments in course scheduling, pedagogical style, and lack of support groups for older students need to be overcome, if education for the elderly is to take off in an aging society. The success of special courses designed for older students and of residential learning suggests that making universities and colleges accessible to older students in the future has great potential, if properly planned. It is also a way for universities to combat the spectre of declining enrolments in an aging population.

The challenges to educational policy in an aging society do not end with the enrolment of more older students in colleges, however. There is an expanding market for ongoing, career-related education and for preretirement education. Such courses have been developed by companies, labour unions and educational institutions. Older people facing retirement have an enormous need to learn more about pensions and annuities, health and wellness, housing options and the aging process itself. Many older people express considerable interest in these matters. There is a further need for the proper training and/or certification of preretirement planners and educators, to ensure a minimal level of competence and to ensure that older people are not abused by untrained teachers or entrepreneurs (Thornton 1983).

Another educational policy issue in an aging society is the need for mass education to dispel myths about aging, as well as myths and misconceptions about population aging. Curriculum supplements and special courses could be devised both inside and outside of schools, colleges and universities. This educational process is already under way in Canada, with the development of centres for research and teaching in gerontology (McPherson 1983, 15-18). Population aging has been targeted as an important research and teaching area by granting agencies of the Canadian government. This initiative has allowed many scholars to engage in research on aging that might otherwise not have been done. It has also enabled some scholars to "re-tool" as gerontologists, and thus to find jobs.

Educational policy in an aging Canada might also encourage greater involvement of retirees in planning for the future. This could take the form, as it has in Saskatchewan, of older people acquiring education in order to assist other older people. It could also take the form of advisory boards of older people who would offer counsel to governments and the private sector on preretirement preparation courses, on pension planning, on housing and other issues of concern to an aging society. Society could draw on older peoples' expertise and, in the process, benefit the older advisors themselves, who would feel useful and wise.

CONCLUSION

In this chapter, only a few of the many complex policy issues resulting from population aging in Canada have been discussed. In considering policy issues in the areas of the economy, retirement and work, health, housing and education, new visions of what can be done have been emphasized. The challenges, policy and otherwise, to planning for an aging society are large but it is expected that, once grasped, they can be met to the betterment of society.

In the next chapter, the future of demographic aging in Canada will be discussed. The need to plan for this future on the basis of what we understand today is imperative, not because an aging population is alarming, but because its needs will be so different.

CHAPTER 6

THE FUTURE OF DEMOGRAPHIC AGING

Population aging is a process that has been under way since before Canada came into existence as a country. It has accelerated over the past two decades as a result of the precipitous decline in the birth rate. Despite the wishful talk of some policy-makers and a few hopeful social scientists, it is unlikely that the present-day trend toward an older population will be turned around. The birth rate is low in Canada now because people prefer to have smaller families. Even if there were an increase in the birth rate as the women of the baby boom generation approached the end of their reproductive lives, this increase would likely be a temporary phenomenon. The overall effect on the inexorable process of demographic aging of such an echo boom or a boomlet, as this upturn in fertility is often termed, would be minimal. It is similarly unlikely, for a variety of reasons (some of them political and economic), that Canada would be willing to increase the annual number of immigrants to the degree necessary to offset the contemporary trend in demographic aging. For these reasons, demographic aging in Canada is here to stay.

It is not possible to consider a long-term trend like demographic aging without reference to what society may look like years down the road. Given that the future has not yet happened, we rely on population projections for our visions of what it might hold. Our analysis here will deal with three areas: major demographic trends such as projected fertility, mortality, and immigration levels and patterns; an examination of the age structure of Canada's population in the future; and an analysis of the relationships that will exist among the principal age groups in the future.

FUTURE CANADIAN TRENDS IN FERTILITY, MORTALITY AND IMMIGRATION

Future patterns of the major demographic variables, including fertility, mortality and immigration, are not easy or straightforward to predict. Nonetheless, it is vital that we attempt to do so, because these variables provide the context in which demographic aging occurs, and affect its pace. Long-term trends in fertility, mortality and immigration also provide the framework in which to anticipate the social, economic and political challenges that may arise as a consequence of demographic aging.

The Future of Fertility

Of the three major demographic processes, fertility is the most variable, the most difficult to explain, and the hardest to predict. It is also the single most important variable in demographic aging. Understanding its dynamics, therefore, is essential to being able to predict the course of demographic aging. Unfortunately, demographers and social scientists do not have an impressive record of predicting fertility trends. The long-term decline in birth rates that began at the time of the industrial revolution had been predicted by demographers in the 1940s to continue unabated. They failed entirely to anticipate the baby boom. In more recent times, demographers did not predict the degree to which fertility in the 1970s and 1980s would decline in North America. Nonetheless, it is crucial to attempt to predict the future pattern of fertility in Canada, since this pattern is closely bound to demographic aging and Canada's future age structure.

Canadian fertility has fluctuated widely during the last century or so. The overall trend, however, has been downward from a very high level of 45.2 births per 1,000 population per year in 1851-61 (Denton, Feaver and Spencer 1980, 4). However inadequate a measure the crude birth rate may be of fertility, the birth rate has undeniably plummeted in recent years to one-third of its 1851 level. This downward trend was fairly consistent from 1851 until World War II, with the birth rate reaching its lowest point, to that time, during the Great Depression years. Interestingly, a birth rate of 22 per 1,000 population in 1937 (Denton, Feaver and Spencer 1980, 5) created concerns about depopulation or the possible advent of negative population growth (Beaujot and McQuillan 1982, 75). There was little reason during the 1930s to believe that there would be a reversal in the long-term downward trend in fertility. During the Second World War, however, the birth rate started to increase again (Denton, Feaver and Spencer 1980, 5). By 1947, it had reached 29 births per 1,000 population (Denton, Feaver and Spencer 1980, 5). The "baby boom" was under way.

People sometimes think that the "baby boom" refers only to the brief period directly following World War II, when a sharp increase in fertility occurred as a result of the return of the soldiers from war. There was undeniably a surge in births in the early postwar years, 1946 and 1947. However, the baby boom period began before the war ended and continued until the beginning of the 1960s. During this entire period of fifteen years or so, the numbers of births rose almost continuously (Beaujot and McQuillan 1982, 54), with the peak of the baby boom occurring in 1956-58 (Statistics Canada 1984b, 13). This created very large generations of people, in fact the largest the world has ever experienced. The size of the birth cohorts during this period has had, and continues to have, an enormous impact on every aspect of Canadian society. A distinct bulge has been produced in the age structure, a bulge that shapes and transforms social and economic institutions. Figure 6.1 gives a graphic indication of this baby boom's size and effects in the future. It is apparent from this that even if the birth rate had not

FIGURE 6.1

POPULATION BY AGE AND SEX, CANADA, 1981, PROJECTED TO 2006 AND 2031
(Low-Growth Scenario)

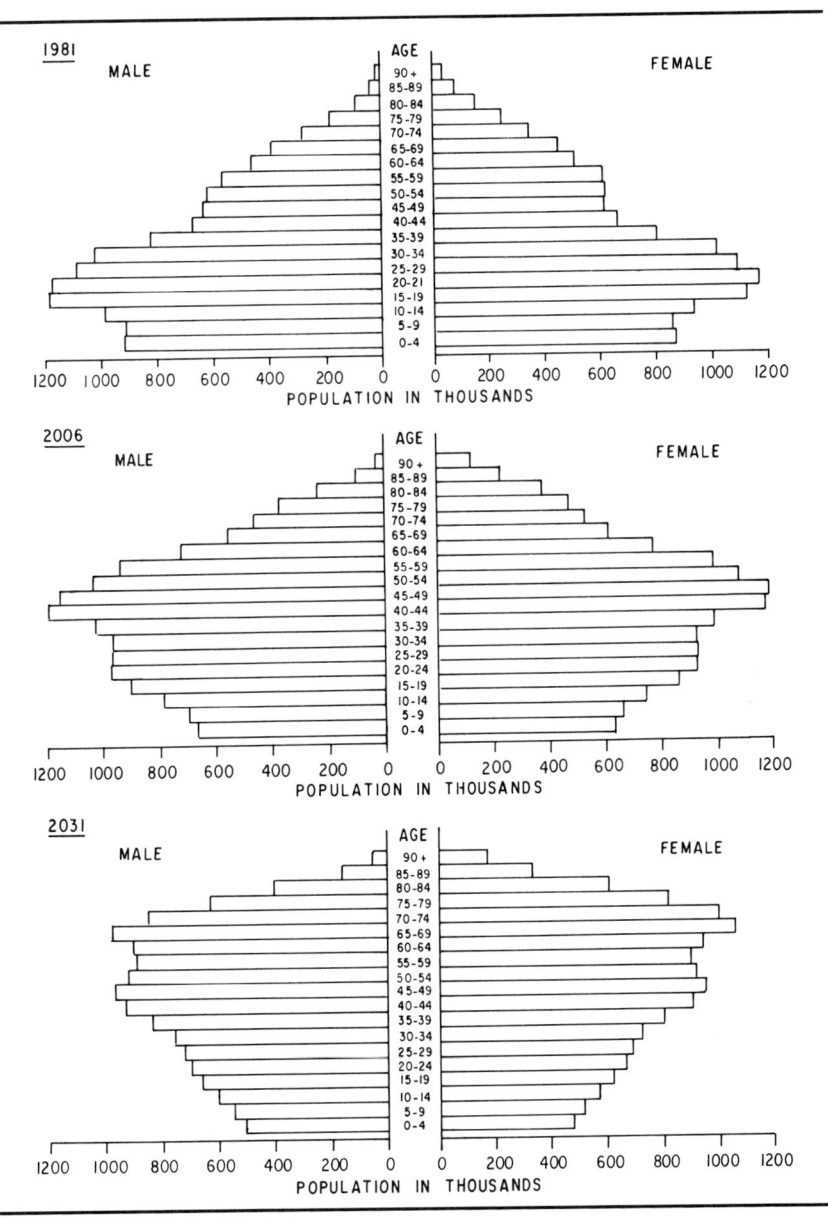

SOURCE: Statistics Canada, *Population Projections for Canada, Provinces and Territories, 1984–2006* (Catalogue No. 91-520), p. 49 (Ottawa: Minister of Supply and Services, 1985).

declined precipitously in the 1970s and 1980s, the baby boom would have remained an important determining force in the shaping of Canada's current age structure.

By 1971, fertility had fallen to below replacement level (Statistics Canada 1984, 73), with an average of 2.1 births per woman. This does not mean that zero population growth had been reached, however. The large numbers of women (from the baby boom generation) of childbearing age in the 1970s means that if each woman had only 2.1 children, the birth rate would still remain high and actually increase. The achievement of zero population growth is very much contingent, therefore, on the age structure of the population or the size of the group of women of childbearing age. Since 1971, much to the surprise of many analysts, the fertility rate has continued to decline. By 1982, it had reached 1.7 children per woman (Statistics Canada 1984b, 122). It is not inappropriate to refer to this recent period as a "baby bust" era (Grindstaff 1975; 1985; Statistics Canada 1984b).

When the baby bust period first began, demographers attributed it, in part, to postponement of births by women who were starting careers or by couples both working to save money so as to provide a better start for their offspring. Other analysts pointed to the invention of the Pill as the cause, although exactly how the Pill works without motivation to have fewer children is unclear. Pill use can be stopped when there is a desire to become pregnant. Historical evidence clearly suggests that the very high birth rates of preindustrial Europe were lowered significantly without access to any modern form of birth control.

The crucial element in fertility decline seems to be a strong motivation to have smaller families rather than anything else (Statistics Canada 1984b). When the motivation is sufficiently strong, the means are somehow found to avoid births, or at least large numbers of births. The fact that the baby bust period has now continued for some 10 plus years has led a Statistics Canada (1984b, 73) report to conclude that postponement is not the major phenomenon being observed: "the rate has remained below the replacement level for each of the past 10 years and there is serious doubt that some cohorts will be able to catch up sufficiently before age 50 to ensure their replacement."

Since 1971 there has been an almost unbroken downward trend in fertility for women up to the age of 28, that is, for women who are biologically the most fertile (Statistics Canada 1984a, 73). Slightly increased fertility among women over 30 offsets only in an insignificant way the decline in fertility among younger women. There has been a distinctly sharp drop in the number of large families in Canada. For example, almost 40 percent of married women born in 1876 or earlier had had at least six children. In the early 1980s the comparable percentage is barely 5 percent (Statistics Canada 1984b, 31). Unlike the low fertility period of the 1930s, there is now no polarization between two groups of couples, one with large families and one with small families (Statistics Canada 1984b, 14). Today, large families have virtually disappeared. As well, recent evidence suggests that there has been and will continue to be a significant rise in voluntary childlessness in Canada (Statistics Canada 1984b, 34). It has been projected that as many as 16 percent of women may forego maternity in Canada (Statistics Canada 1984b, 33).

Given the pattern of later childbearing, smaller families, the virtual disappearance of large families, and the likelihood of increasing voluntary childlessness, it seems that low fertility is likely to be a reality on the Canadian scene for some time in the future (Gee 1981; Grindstaff 1985). It seems to represent a clear preference on the part of Canadians for a radical departure from preexisting beliefs about the importance of reproduction, family and even the purpose of marriage.

Given the complexity of modern fertility trends and patterns in Canada, what is likely to happen to fertility in the future? There is considerable debate about this. Some analysts believe that the present levels of extremely low fertility represent the clear social and economic preferences of couples today. Others argue that, although not a temporary trend, the current low fertility levels may be turned upward again as baby boom generation women approach the end of their reproductive lives (Statistics Canada 1984b, 113). Some fluctuations in fertility levels do indeed seem to be characteristic of most modern societies that practise effective contraception. However, it would seem that the trend toward low fertility in Canada is unlikely to reverse itself, at least in the immediate future. Any swings in levels in the future are likely to be of smaller magnitude than they have been in the past.

The fluxes and flows in the birth rate in Canada have created an age structure that will remain with us for many years. The 1960s saw a vast expansion in the educational system in Canada to accommodate the baby boom generation's educational requirements. The 1970s and 1980s are a time of school closings and concern about population aging. There is little doubt that when the baby boom generation retires in the 2020s, it will have as profound an effect on the social and economic institutions that cater to the older population as it did on the educational institutions of the 1960s, 1970s and 1980s. However, these institutions likely will recover and survive, as did education. They may even be improved as a consequence of the increased demand.

It may be that there will be a mini-boom in births as the baby boom generation makes a last effort to reproduce before it becomes too late biologically. It seems clear, however, that present-day low fertility represents a shift from the past in the values surrounding parenthood and reproduction. It is equally clear, however, that the age structure anomalies produced by an historically fluctuating birth rate in the past have undeniable implications for population aging far into the future.

The Future of Mortality

Mortality is also an important variable in demographic aging, but generally less important than fertility. As was seen in Chapter 4, the role of mortality in demographic aging is larger in countries with very high life expectancies. The reason for this is that in these countries the probability of survival at young ages is already approaching 100 percent, so that any improvements in mortality tend to affect those at older ages more. It is in demographically older countries, such as Canada, that mortality contributes more to demographic aging than in countries with lower life expectancies.

The crude death rate (deaths per 1,000 population) in Canada has been falling since 1851-61 (Denton, Feaver and Spencer 1980, 6). However, in recent times, the rate of decline has slowed considerably. In fact the 1971-76 death rate in Canada was virtually the same as the rate in 1966-71 (Denton, Feaver and Spencer 1980, 6). By 1982, this rate of approximately 7.2 deaths per 1,000 population had dropped to 6.9 (Statistics Canada 1984a, 81). These very low death rates are predicted to increase in the future as the proportion of older persons in the population increases (Statistics Canada 1984a, 81). If any improvements are made in mortality rates in the future, these are likely to have only a moderate impact, given that the rates are so low at present (Statistics Canada 1985, 23).

For the purpose of attempting to predict the future age structure and the degree and pace of demographic aging, it is more important to analyze life expectancy trends and trends in age-specific mortality, than to focus on crude death rate trends. Life expectancy is calculated from a life table that summarizes mortality rates (the inverse of which is the probability of surviving) by age. Usually life tables begin in one year and show age-specific death rates applied to a hypothetical population of 100,000 persons until all members of this population have died. It is a rather simple mathematical calculation, then, to predict how many years a person of a given age is likely to live under the prevailing death rates of a given year (see Foot 1982, 50-54). Life tables have been available in Canada since the 1931 Census. They are usually constructed separately for men and for women since there are such dramatic mortality differences between the sexes.

Life expectancy in Canada for both men and women has increased continuously since 1931. Men have gained an average of 11.9 years, increasing their life expectancy from 60.0 in 1931 (Foot 1982, 55) to 71.9 in 1980-82 (Statistics Canada 1984, 82-84). The greatest gains in life expectancy, contrary to popular belief, have been made at the younger ages, particularly during the first year of life.

Differences in life expectancies between men and women have persisted in Canada since 1931. Women in Canada have always lived longer than men. The difference in 1931 was 2.1 years. By 1976, it was 7.3 years (Denton, Feaver and Spencer 1980, 6). A slight closing of the gap in life expectancy between men and women occurred between 1976 and 1981, to 7.1 years (Statistics Canada 1984a, 84).

In the decade of the 1970s in Canada, particularly in the latter half, rapid gains were made in life expectancy. In the five-year period from 1971 to 1976, male life expectancy increased by more than it had throughout the entire decade of the 1960s (Foot 1982, 54-55). More rapid gains were made in the life expectancy of men over the 1976-81 period than in the previous five-year period (Statistics Canada 1984a, 81-83). Female life expectancy also improved in the 1970s, but somewhat less spectacularly than for males (Statistics Canada 1984a, 82-84). In the second half of the 1970s, a significant change occurred in the contributing causes of improved life expectancy for both sexes. Infant mortality, the chief contributor to improved life chances in the past, continued to decline. Significantly, however, improvements were made in survival probability at the older ages. For men, for example, survival probability started to increase after age 35 but dropped slightly at more advanced ages. Women's survival probability improvements were small until age 60, at which time they rose sharply (Statistics Canada 1984a, 83-84).

The gains made recently in life expectancy of Canadians seem to be in contradiction to the often-made observation that death rates in the developed world have reached their lowest possible levels. An additional sentiment often heard is that any further reductions in mortality are likely to be small. This may be one of the apparent paradoxes of an aging society. Death rates are low in Canada and not likely to become much lower. Despite this, however, due largely to recent reductions in deaths attributable to cardiovascular disease, gains continue to be made in life expectancy. These gains are made in improving survival chances for those who are older (men above 35, women above 60), however, rather than by improving life chances of children, teenagers, young adult men or women of middle age. This results in aging at the top or apex of the population. In other words, more older people are surviving longer. The gains of the 1970s may be short-term, however, as the Canadian population continues to reach its biological potential in terms of life span. Even if life expectancy continues to be very high, in an aging society death rates inevitably go up.

The Future of International Migration

Throughout Canada's history, immigration has played a major role in the country's population dynamics. Although the net contribution of immigration has varied over the years, it has always been important. At times, however, emigration (or outmigration) from Canada has offset the effects of immigration. Most notably, this outmigration has included both Canadians *and* immigrants to Canada who subsequently migrate to the United States. Although accurate records are kept on the number of immigrants who come to Canada, there are no records at all on who leaves Canada for another country. Thus, we must rely on estimation techniques.

The highest rates of immigration to Canada occurred during the first decade of the twentieth century. On a gross population basis, the rate of immigration then was equal to 25 percent of the average population of that period (Denton, Feaver and Spencer 1980, 6). Many of the early immigrants to Canada had very large families; those children are now entering the ranks of the elderly in Canada in large numbers. Further, due to that wave of immigration, more members of the older population (compared to the younger population) speak neither English nor French at home (Health and Welfare Canada 1983, 28). Many of these older people reside in the Prairie provinces, where the early immigrants tended to settle. Clearly, immigration is important in contemporary patterns of aging (Health and Welfare Canada 1983, 28).

Net immigration to Canada fell precipitously during and after the First World War. (Net immigration is the total gain in population due to migration, once outmigrants are considered.) During the Depression years, Canada had a net loss of population due to emigration (Denton, Feaver and Spencer 1980, 6). The World War II period again saw large numbers of immigrants coming to Canada. This high level of immigration continued through the 1951–61 period, during which net immigration peaked (Denton, Feaver and Spencer 1980, 6, 8). In fact, during the 1951–61 period, net immigration actually exceeded that of the 1901–11 period (Denton, Feaver and Spencer 1980, 9). However, immigration made a larger relative contribution to population growth in the earlier period than in the 1950s, because the Canadian population was much smaller early in the century.

Since people who immigrate are often young adults, typically between 20 and 30 years old, the net immigration of the 1950s was sufficiently high to make an impact on the ranks of today's retired population. Those immigrating to Canada in the 1950s would have been born in the 1920s and 1930s. Thus, the oldest group of these immigrants would turn 65 in 1985–86, with the youngest group retiring in the early part of the next century. On the other hand, at the time they arrived in Canada, these 1950s immigrants contributed to the relative youthfulness of the population, and added further to this youthfulness by having children.

During the 1951–61 period, immigrants tended to be disproportionately male. Subsequent immigration flows to Canada have been more sex-balanced (Foot 1980, 58–59).

The 1970s and early 1980s have seen enormous fluctuations in the number of immigrants admitted from year to year. For example, a peak was reached in 1974 with 219,000 immigrants being admitted to Canada, comparable to the all-time high of 282,000 in 1957 (Statistics Canada 1984a, 91–92). In 1978, however, only 80,000 immigrants were admitted (Statistics Canada 1984b, 93). The main factor behind these fluctuations is the changing federal immigration policy. On average, in recent years Canada has annually added approximately 150,000 people to its population through immigration (including refugees).

Generally, the effect of immigration on the age structure has been to contribute to its youthfulness, by decreasing the median age of the population and contributing new youngsters. It should be noted, however, that the age structure of immigrants has also been changing. The median age of both male and female immigrants rose (from 25.5 to 27.8 for males and from 26.3 to 30 for females) during the 1970-80 period (Statistics Canada 1984a, 96). In 1980, recent immigrants were generally older than those who arrived in 1970. This phenomenon is explained in part by the Canadian government's policy of family reunification. Once the younger immigrants are settled, they sponsor their older relatives. This humanitarian policy has added, but only in small measure, to the numbers of older people in Canada in the 1980s and 1990s.

Predicting the future picture of immigration is certainly more difficult than predicting mortality trends (but perhaps less difficult than predicting future fertility). Immigration levels are determined by the vagaries of government administrations under the umbrella of economic pressures. Canadian immigration policy has long been recognized as self-serving (Beaujot and McQuillan 1982, 109). Immigration policy has been and continues to be defined in terms of "what immigrants can do for Canada" (Hawkins 1972). Canada's immigration policy in the past has been pegged rather directly to Canada's economic goals (Taylor 1978). For example, the need to settle the West led to the immigration of the early 1900s. The second large wave of immigrants in the 1950s was composed of people recruited for their qualifications to help in Canada's economic development. We could cite many other examples of fine-tuning of the immigration policy to better serve the needs of the Canadian economy (see Taylor 1978 and Hawkins 1972). In the light of present and past experience with immigration in Canada, it seems likely that immigration levels will be kept relatively modest (Denton, Feaver and Spencer 1980, 24).

Given present concerns about the growing older population, as well as international pressures on Canada to accept more immigrants (Hawkins 1985), it is conceivable that immigration policy could be seen as the means to solve the "problem" of demographic aging. Exactly how many new immigrants would be required each year to offset the demographic aging process is not clear, but it is doubtful if Canada would be willing to increase the numbers sufficiently to accomplish this goal.

CANADA'S AGE STRUCTURE IN THE FUTURE

The fluctuating trends of fertility, mortality and immigration, past and present, leave an inexorable pattern on the shape of a population, just as footprints left in wet cement remain long after the cement dries. The pattern thus formed is the population's age-sex structure. In this section, Canada's present age-sex structure is examined and analyzed as to its implications for demographic aging. The present structure is then projected into the future to allow an analysis of the dimensions of demographic aging that lie ahead for Canada.

Implications of Canada's Present Age-Sex Structure

The age-sex structure of a population at a given point in time is typically depicted by a population pyramid, a back-to-back bar graph showing males and females separately (see Chapter 1). The bars usually represent five-year age groups, but can be single years. These graphs provide, in one glance, a history of the population's demographic experience. A broad stubby pyramid manifests a large birth rate and high death rate with low life expectancy. A country that has experienced enormous losses of men due to a war, as did the U.S.S.R. during World War II, will have a visible indentation on the male side of the pyramid at the crucial ages. Similarly, a country that has experienced net gains due to immigration, as did Canada particularly in the 1901-11 and 1951-61 periods, will show bumps in the age pyramid for the relevant age groups of immigrants.

Canada's 1981 age-sex structure, as shown in the top pyramid in Figure 6.1, clearly attests to the country's past experiences with fertility, mortality and immigration. Most striking in the 1981 population pyramid is the rapid transition from baby boom to baby bust. People aged 15-39 in 1981 form the bulge of the age pyramid. Their presence in schools in 1968 caused enrolments to peak (Beaujot and McQuillan 1982, 135). By 1976, school enrolments had dropped by 22 percent (Beaujot and McQuillan 1982, 135). Similar enrolment drops are on the immediate horizon for postsecondary educational institutions, as the baby boom generation moves out of university.

The baby bust period, begun 10-15 years prior to 1981, shows in the age-sex pyramid as a shrunken generation. A tiny group of people seems to lie in the shadow of the largest generation the world has ever experienced. Although Canadian fertility has now hit an historic low, the indented bottom of the population pyramid in 1981 is characteristic of many modern industrial societies. As a population experiences lowered birth rates for a prolonged period, the pattern of demographic aging manifests itself in a *rectangularization* of the population pyramid.

Even though Canada's 1981 population pyramid in no way resembles a rectangle, its classic, pyramidal shape is changing. No longer is it characterized by the wide base and gently sloping sides of a young population. As a population ages, it seems to gain a "spare tire" around the middle (a pattern not unknown to many aging individuals).

The economic and social significance of the sudden, sharp and prolonged decline in the birth rate in Canada in the 1970s and 1980s may become most apparent in the 2020s and 2030s, when the baby boom generation hits retirement and old age. At this time, the small baby bust generation will be called upon for support. Given this imbalance in size between the work force and the older population, there might be a strain. Alternatively, it might be that patterns of work and retirement (as discussed in Chapter 5) would be sufficiently transformed so that many baby boom generation people would, in fact, support other baby boomers in their retirement.

It is clear that the rate of population growth has begun to decline, with the end of the baby boom era. This decline in population growth rate has concerned many analysts, who associate it with a decline in economic growth rates. Close examination of the 1981 Canadian population pyramid, however, shows that the long-term rate of decline in population growth may be falsely inflated to some extent. The period of the baby boom was also marked by a particularly healthy rate of net immigration during the 1950s, hence the rapid growth rate in Canada. It seems almost inevitable that this very high rate of growth would even out eventually. The surprise was that it turned around so very quickly, and gave way to the lowest birth rate level in Canada's history.

Looking only at short-run trends in the birth rate might lead to the conclusion that Canada is experiencing a precipitous drop in population growth. However, if the baby boom period is defined not as the standard of population growth, but as a somewhat anomalous period, then the drop in the rate of population growth may be viewed as less precipitous and may cause less concern.

There is one aspect of the relationship between the baby boom and baby bust generations, even in 1981, that some analysts believe might offset their predictions of zero population growth and accelerated population aging in the future. The women of the baby boom generation are now beginning to arrive at their last years of reproduction. Some of them may be late childbearers, since the birth rate among women over 30 is increasing (Statistics Canada 1984b, 27). Researchers, however, note only a slight, largely negligible adjustment in the fertility rate of women over 30 (Grindstaff 1984).

Additionally, there are so many baby boom women of childbearing age that, even if they maintain a low birth rate and small family sizes, the actual numbers of children in the population can increase. This is known as population growth momentum. The population continues to grow despite much lowered birth rates because of the momentum built into the age structure (Statistics Canada 1984b, 24). There was evidence in 1983 that this is already occurring. The steady downward decline in the birth *rate* has masked the slight increase in the actual *number* of children, particularly pre-school age children (Statistics Canada 1984a, 37). Since 1976, when the last group of baby boom generation women began having children, the numbers of children aged 0–5 have been increasing (Statistics Canada 1984a, 37). This in no way signals a reversal in the fertility trend but is due to the age structure, i.e. because of the size of the generation of potential mothers, the growth in numbers of pre-school children at present partially offsets the decline in school-age population. This large group of 1981 pre-schoolers may also be important in the future as supporters of the retired baby boomers.

The merit of the population pyramid lies in its capacity to reveal at a glance the past and the future of population aging. The future of population aging in Canadian society will not be entirely surprising, since it is revealed in the population pyramid of 1981. The older people of Canada's tomorrow are the young and middle-aged people of today. Given present levels of mortality and high levels of life expectancy, these people are not likely to disappear, nor, given Canada's past experience, are they likely to emigrate in large numbers.

Canada's Future Age-Sex Structure

The age-sex structure of the future will depend on the future course of the basic demographic forces — fertility, mortality and immigration. As we have seen, all three forces are the complex products of multiple social and economic trends, and thus subject to change. As a result, predicting their future course with a high degree of certainty is difficult. On the other hand, certain aspects of fertility, mortality and immigration have been analyzed and are well understood. This allows for prediction within a relatively narrow range. The projections we will discuss here are based on methods of projection devised and carried out by some of the best demographers in Canada (who have access to sophisticated trend analysis of the three basic variables, as well as to the most recent data). It should be remembered, however, that demographers' predictions in the past have been wrong. The baby boom was not anticipated, nor was the recent sharp decline in fertility.

The future age structure of any population depends, to a large degree, on the future course of fertility. (The patterns of mortality and immigration also matter, but to a much lesser degree.) The challenge is that fertility is the least amenable to prediction of the three variables. If errors are made in projecting the future age-sex structure of Canada, or the *degree* of demographic aging to be expected, these errors would probably be due to incorrect fertility projection. Given this, and the fact that there has been much speculation about what will happen to Canada's fertility rate in the future, most projections allow for at least three possible ranges of fertility — a high, a medium and a low range. The most recent Statistics Canada projections, from which much of our data here are drawn, are based on the most likely future scenario — an assumption of continued low fertility.

When the future age structure is referred to, it is generally taken to mean the entire age structure as represented by the population pyramid. The numbers of those who will be 65 in, say, 20 years' time are known now, barring any enormous change in current patterns of either mortality or immigration. The proportion that will be constituted by the population over the age of 65 cannot be known with full certainty, because of possible future influences on the birth rate. The further we project into the future, the greater the uncertainty of the projections. As Havens correctly points out:

> ... when someone says that the population 65 or over will constitute 15 per cent or 18 per cent of the population of Canada by the year 2011 or by the year 2031, one must be wary. Such a statement is based on imputing fertility behaviour to the grandchildren of the Baby Boom, i.e. to the children of those who are not yet born. Predicting or projecting fertility behaviour for that group is at best risky and at worst unreliable (Havens 1981, 10).

Despite the riskiness involved, projections of age structures are necessary in order to plan adequately.

Keeping all these precautions in mind, let us examine what the future may hold for Canada in terms of age-sex structure. Figure 6.1, referred to earlier, shows a 1981 age-sex pyramid and projected pyramids for 2006 and 2031. These projections are based on the following assumptions made by Statistics Canada: (1) the total fertility rate (number of children per woman at the end of reproduction) will continue to decline from 1.7 in 1981 to a low of 1.4 by 1996 and will remain constant thereafter (Statistics Canada 1985, 18); (2) the total level of immigration will stabilize at 50,000 net gain of immigrants a year and will remain constant at that level (Statistics Canada 1985, 31, 41); (3) future changes in life expectancy will be lower in future than those observed for 1976–81; (4) the male-female difference will narrow; (5) the similarity between mortality levels of males and females at very young and very old ages will continue (Statistics Canada 1985, 26–27). These assumptions underlie the low-growth scenario projection by Statistics Canada.

From the pyramids presented in Figure 6.1, it is apparent that, if these assumptions hold, Canadian society in the future will be substantially different than it is today. The aging process, begun in the nineteenth century, will continue and accelerate. For example, the median age of the Canadian population will rise from 30 years in 1983 to 41 years in 2006 and reach 48 years by 2031 (Statistics Canada 1985, 48). This change is illustrated in the dramatic shift that is seen to occur in the shape of the age pyramid over the 50 years portrayed in Figure 6.1. The pyramid changes from being relatively bottom-heavy to being top-heavy. Among electors, for example, 14 percent in 1981 are above the age of 65. By 2006, the comparable proportion will be 18 percent and by 2031, it will be 31 percent (Statistics Canada 1985, 50). A slowdown in the rate of population growth is also apparent over the projection period, reaching zero around 2006 and declining thereafter (Statistics Canada 1985, 43). Among the most dramatic shifts portrayed in the low-growth scenario of Figure 6.1 is the growth in the proportion of the population over the age of 65.

In Table 6.1, this low-growth scenario is compared with the high-growth

TABLE 6.1

**PERCENTAGE OF POPULATION 65 YEARS AND OVER
CANADA, 1981, AND PROJECTED TO 2031
(Low- and High-Growth Scenarios)**

| | Percentage of Population 65 Years and Over ||
	Low-Growth	High-Growth
1981	9.7	9.7
1986	10.7	10.6
1991	11.9	11.7
1996	13.1	12.4
2001	14.0	12.8
2006	14.7	13.0
2011	16.1	13.6
2016	18.4	15.0
2021	21.0	16.4
2026	23.9	17.9
2031	26.6	18.9

NOTE: Low-growth scenario is based on an assumption of 1.4 children per woman by 1996; high-growth scenario is based on an assumption of 2.20 children per woman by 1996.

SOURCE: Statistics Canada, *Population Projections for Canada, Provinces and Territories, 1984-2006* (Catalogue No. 91-520), Table 14, p. 48 (Ottawa: Minister of Supply and Services, 1985).

scenario to see the effects of varying assumptions on demographic aging. The high-growth scenario assumes the same rate as the low-growth scenario for mortality; immigration is to remain constant at 100,000 a year, and fertility constant at 2.2 children per woman after 1996. Under the low-growth assumption, it is clear that the proportion of the population aged 65 and over would grow at a very rapid pace. By 2016, for example, it would have doubled what it was in 1981. By 2031, more than one-quarter of Canada's population would be 65 and over. In numbers, this means that there would be over 7 million older people in Canada by the first third of the twenty-first century (Statistics Canada 1985, 57). This is almost one-third of Canada's 1981 population. The high-growth scenario also shows a rapid growth in the proportion made up of older people, but a less dramatic growth than under the low-growth scenario. By 2031, under the high-growth scenario, there would be a doubling of the proportion 65 years and over from the 1981 level.

From the above discussion, it should be apparent that the low-growth scenario, or some variation of it, is more likely to become the reality in Canada than is the high-growth scenario. It therefore seems realistic to anticipate that approximately one-quarter of Canada's population in fifty years' time will be comprised of people over the age of 65.

A second large change in the age structure of Canada's future population occurs with the working age population. Under the low-growth scenario, portrayed in the population pyramids (Figure 6.1) it is clear that the working age population will constitute a larger percentage of the total population as the fertility rate declines, at least in the short run. This is particularly evident in the 2006 pyramid. By 2031, however, as the proportion of older persons exceeds the proportion of younger persons, it seems from the pyramid that the working age population might constitute about the same proportion as it does in 1981.

Table 6.2 enables a quantification of this general trend under the low-growth scenario, and a comparison with the high-growth scenario. Indeed, the percentage of the population in the working ages, under low-growth assumptions, rises steadily until 2006 and 2011, at which time it slowly declines. By 2031, this percentage is somewhat smaller than it is in 1981. Under the high-growth scenario, there are only small changes in the working age proportion until after 2016, when it begins to decline. Even by 2031, however, the percentage of working age population is only 2 percent lower under the high-growth scenario than under the low-growth scenario. This essentially means that, whatever path fertility takes in the future, there is not likely to be a major change in the proportion in working ages over the next fifty years.

TABLE 6.2

PERCENTAGE OF POPULATION IN WORKING AGES FOR CANADA, 1981, AND PROJECTED TO 2031
(Low- and High-Growth Scenarios)

	Percentage of Population Aged 18–64	
	Low-Growth Scenario	High-Growth Scenario
1981	62.2	62.2
1986	63.6	63.6
1991	63.8	63.1
1996	64.2	62.1
2001	65.3	61.6
2006	66.6	61.7
2011	66.6	61.7
2016	65.0	60.8
2021	62.8	59.4
2026	60.5	57.7
2031	58.5	56.5

NOTE: Low-growth scenario is based on an assumption of 1.4 children per woman by 1996; high-growth scenario is based on an assumption of 2.20 children per woman by 1996.

SOURCE: Statistics Canada, *Population Projections for Canada, Provinces and Territories, 1984–2006* (Catalogue No. 91–520), Table 17, p. 54 (Ottawa: Minister of Supply and Services, 1985).

FIGURE 6.2

PERCENTAGES OF TOTAL POPULATION IN SELECTED AGE GROUPS, CANADA, 1951 TO 2021

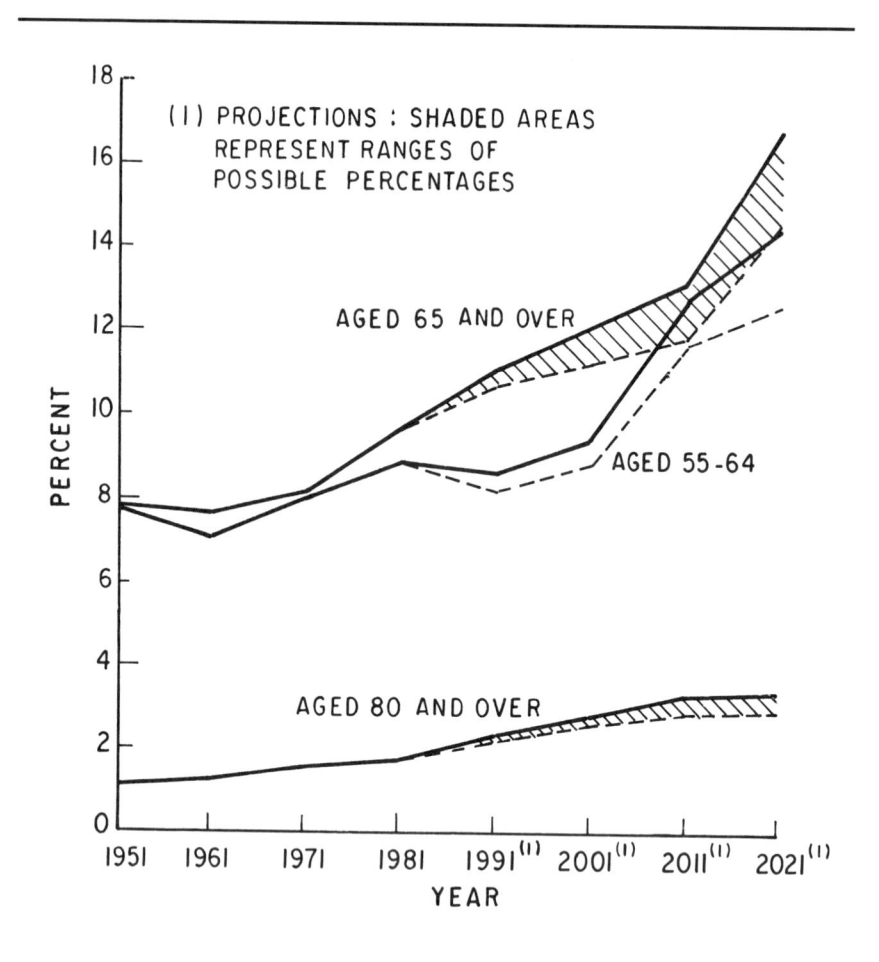

[1] The "high-growth" scenario here, in fact, is based on a growth rate just above replacement level. This is a much lower rate of growth than occurred in Canada during the Depression years.

NOTE: Shaded areas represent ranges of possible percentages for projections.
SOURCE: Canada. 1983. *Fact Book on Aging in Canada*. Ottawa: Minister of Supply and Services Canada. P. 17.

FIGURE 6.3
RATIO OF FEMALES TO MALES IN SELECTED AGE GROUPS, CANADA, 1951 TO 2001

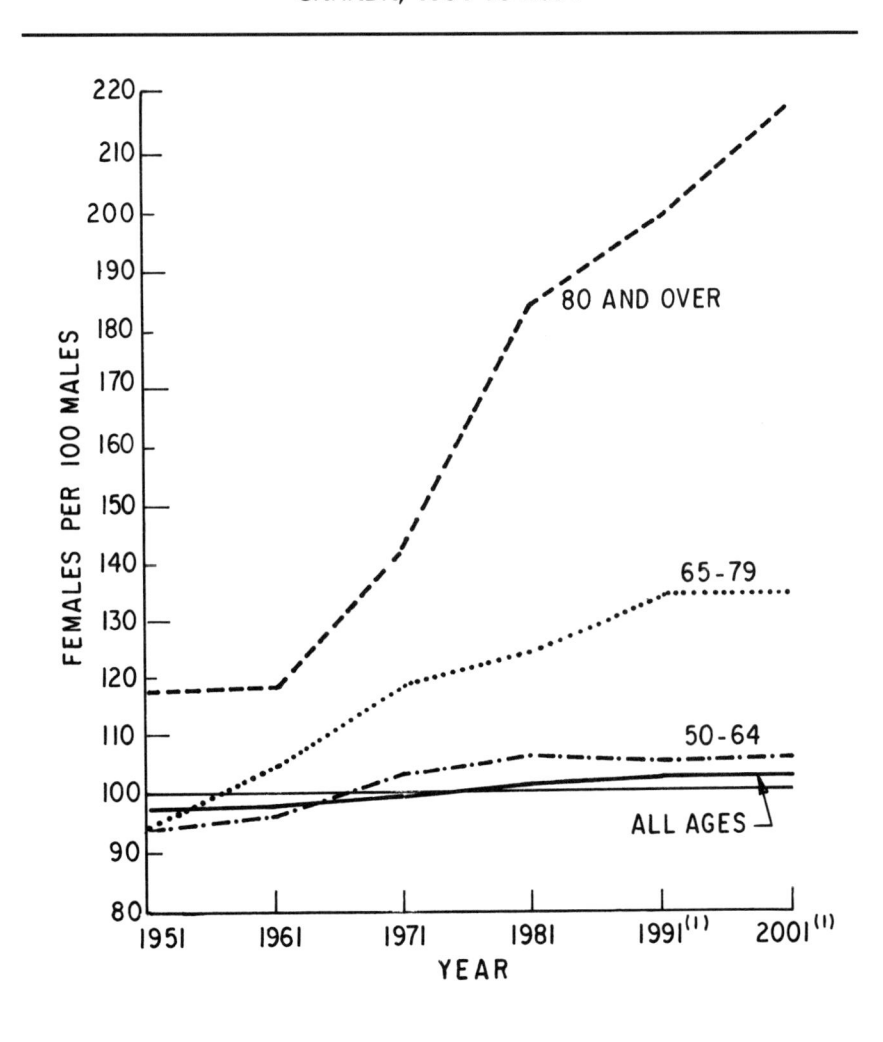

[1] The "high-growth" scenario here, in fact, is based on a growth rate just above replacement level. This is a much lower rate of growth than occurred in Canada during the Depression years.

SOURCE: Canada. 1983. *Fact Book on Aging in Canada.* Ottawa: Minister of Supply and Services Canada. P. 21.

A close examination of the projected population pyramids in Figure 6.1 reveals a fairly dramatic change in the age and sex composition of the older population. At older ages, the bars get longer on the female side of the pyramid. As well, the very old population grows, relative to the younger old population. In Figure 6.3, it is evident that the proportion of the population 80 years and over has grown even more dramatically than the proportion 65 years and over. In future, this oldest group is expected to grow even more. In Figure 6.2, as well, both the future growth of the proportion 65 and over and the fluctuation and ultimate growth of the preretirement age group, 55–64, are apparent. In Figure 6.3, the widening numerical imbalance to be expected in the future between men and women becomes vivid. In the mid-twentieth century, males slightly outnumbered females in Canada. By 1971, the sex ratio was in balance for Canadians of all ages. Among the older groups, women have always predominated. What is striking is the degree to which women, particularly women over 80, will predominate in the future. The future of demographic aging in Canada, as in most demographically older countries, has a female face.

TABLE 6.3

PERCENTAGE OF THE POPULATION 65 YEARS AND OVER FOR CANADA AND PROVINCES, 1981, 1991, 2006
(Low-Growth Scenario)

	1981	1991	2006
Canada	9.7	11.9	14.7
Newfoundland	8.1	9.3	11.3
Prince Edward Island	12.2	13.1	14.3
Nova Scotia	10.9	12.7	14.4
New Brunswick	10.3	11.8	13.4
Quebec	8.8	11.3	14.7
Ontario	10.1	12.4	15.5
Manitoba	11.9	13.5	15.3
Saskatchewan	12.0	13.3	13.8
Alberta	7.3	9.3	12.1
British Columbia	10.9	13.2	15.8
Yukon	2.7	5.9	8.9
Northwest Territories	2.9	4.7	9.1

NOTE: Low-growth scenario is based on an assumption of 1.4 children per woman by 1996.

SOURCES: Statistics Canada, *Population Projections for Canada, Provinces and Territories, 1984–2006* (Catalogue No. 91–520), (Ottawa: Minister of Supply and Services, 1985). 1991 data: Table D.3, p. 121; 2006 data: Table D.3, p. 151. 1981 data: Statistics Canada, *1981 Census of Canada* (Catalogue No. 92–901), (Ottawa: Minister of Supply and Services, 1982).

Predicting the age structure of populations at the provincial level is even more difficult than predicting national futures. This is because of the highly unstable and economically sensitive factor of interprovincial migration (Northcott 1984). Statistics Canada, however, has projected provincial age structure into the future, although not as far as for the Canadian population as a whole. This has been done on the basis of extrapolation of past trends and patterns of internal migration (Statistics Canada 1985, 36). Table 6.3 shows a summary of the projected provincial changes for 1981 until 2006 in the population proportion 65 and over.

There is enormous variability from province to province in the projected pace of demographic aging, measured in this way. The provinces experiencing the most rapid growth in their populations 65 years and over, Quebec and Ontario, were not among the oldest in 1981. That distinction goes to Prince Edward Island, Manitoba and Saskatchewan. By 2006, however, the demographically oldest provinces are British Columbia, Ontario and Manitoba. Provinces experiencing the slowest rates of aging during the 1981–2006 period, other than the two territories, are Saskatchewan and Prince Edward Island, two of the oldest provinces demographically in 1981, but also Newfoundland, one of the youngest provinces in 1981. Newfoundland will continue to remain one of the youngest provinces, even in the future. The economic difficulties experienced by this province attest to the clear lack of relationship between youthful age structure and economic well-being. The diversity of projected patterns from province to province suggests the complex interplay of declining birth rates, interprovincial migration, immigration streams, and varying patterns of employment opportunity on the process of demographic aging.

Canada's Future Age Group Relationships

In order to understand the future pattern of demographic aging, it is important that we not only make projections of the age structure, but that we also analyze the shifting ratios and relationships that result from moving the age structure forward in time. As we have seen, Canada's present age structure is very much a product of an enormously fluctuating birth rate, but is also due to surges in immigration. Analyzing the relationships of generations to each other, as projected into the future, allows a better grasp of the dynamics of cohort flow. It further permits an understanding of some of the social and economic implications of population aging, not in the abstract, but with reference to Canada's particular population profile.

Table 6.4 shows dependency ratios for Canada projected to the year 2051, according to an "old population" and a "young population" set of assumptions. (The assumptions are spelled out at the bottom of the table.) Basically, the dependency ratio is a measure of economic burden of the young and the old on those of working ages. Historically, in Canada, the

TABLE 6.4

**TOTAL DEPENDENCY RATIOS (Total Population/20-64)
FOR CANADA, 1976, 1981, AND PROJECTED TO 2051
(Old and Young Population Projections)**

	Total Dependency Ratio	
	Old Population	Young Population
1976	1.80	1.80
1981	1.70	1.75
1986	1.63	1.76
1991	1.61	1.83
1996	1.60	1.90
2001	1.58	1.88
2006	1.56	1.82
2011	1.56	1.81
2016	1.59	1.86
2021	1.64	1.92
2026	1.71	1.95
2031	1.77	1.94
2036	1.79	1.90
2041	1.79	1.87
2046	1.79	1.88
2051	1.80	1.90

NOTE: "Old population" projection is based on low fertility (based on continuance of a 1984 Total Fertility Rate of 1,489 live births per 1000 women), low mortality (projected from a 1971 life-table base, 1.5x1951-1971 changes for the 1971-1991 projections and .75x1951-1971 changes for the 1991-2051 projections) and medium net immigration (80,000 in 1981 projected to continue). "Young population" projection is based on high fertility (based on continuance of a 1984 Total Fertility Rate of 2,979 live births per 1000 women), high mortality (projected from a 1971 life-table base, .5x1951-1971 changes for the 1971-1991 projections and .25x1951-1971 changes for the 1991-2051 projections) and medium net immigration (80,000 in 1981 projected to continue).

SOURCE: Frank T. Denton, Christine M. Feaver and Byron G. Spencer, *The Future Population and Labour Force of Canada: Projections to the Year 2051*. (A study prepared for the Economic Council of Canada), data from Table 5.6, p. 33; assumptions from Chapter 4, pp. 19-27 (Ottawa: Minister of Supply and Services, 1980).

overall dependency ratio has often exceeded 2 (Denton, Feaver and Spencer 1980, 33). In the modern era, it has gone down somewhat, but never below 1.79. Under both old and young population projections, as shown in Table 6.4, there is some variability in the ratios, but at the end of the projection period, in 2051, under the old population projection, the dependency ratio is identical to what it was in 1976. For the young population projection, it is slightly higher than it was in 1976. According to the old population projection (the more likely of the two, given the low fertility rates that we anticipate to continue) the total dependency ratio reaches a low point of 1.56 in 2006 and 2011 and slowly returns to its 1976 level after some 40 years. This is due to the low birth rate, which by this time will have remained low for a long time. The young population projection sees the total dependency ratio hovering between the high 1.70's and the low 1.90's throughout the projection period.

It should be emphasized here that at no time in the next half century, if these projections are correct, will Canada experience the levels of dependency it bore in the nineteenth century. Secondly, no matter what shifts occur in the age structure in the future, no dramatic changes can be anticipated in the overall dependency ratios, even in the distant future. This is true either if fertility remains at the present low or if fertility rates go up. If fertility rates remain low, as in the old population projection, the total dependency ratio will fall considerably by 2016 before it begins to climb again. Of course, the nature of the dependency is obscured in an analysis of total dependency ratios. For this reason, we now turn to an analysis of the trends in the components of dependency as projected into the future.

In Table 6.5, the crossover pattern of young and old age dependency ratios becomes clear. In 1971 in Canada, the total dependency ratio (measured here in a different way than in Table 6.4) was 77.8. By 2031, it is 76.6. This seems not to be much of a difference. However, in 1971, almost two-thirds of the total ratio was composed of children, while in 2031, it is predicted that over half will be composed of older people. Total dependency reaches a low point around 2011, at which time youth and older folks contribute almost equally to total dependency.

TABLE 6.5

YOUTH, OLD AGE AND TOTAL DEPENDENCY RATIOS FOR CANADA, 1971, 1981, AND PROJECTED TO 2031
(Low-Growth Scenario)

	Youth Dependency Ratio (0-17/18-64)	Old Age Dependency Ratio (65+/18-64)	Total Ratio (0-17, 65+)/(18-64)
1971	63.4	14.4	77.8
1981	45.2	15.6	60.8
1991	37.1	21.6	58.7
2001	30.9	24.4	55.2
2011	25.3	27.4	52.7
2021	25.2	37.8	63.0
2031	25.0	51.6	76.6

NOTE: Low-growth scenario is based on an assumption of 1.4 children per woman by 1996.
SOURCE: Statistics Canada, *Population Projections for Canada, Provinces and Territories, 1984-2006* (Catalogue No. 91-520), Table 18, p. 35 (Ottawa: Minister of Supply and Services, 1985).

CONCLUSION

It is clear from this brief look at the relationships among age groups in the future that changes are on the horizon in Canada. The peculiar pattern of a baby boom followed by a baby bust has created a situation in Canada, as in many other places in the industrialized Western world, in which the transition from a youthful society to an older society can be made gracefully. In fact, if we consider that total dependency is projected to reach an all-time historic low in Canada in 2011 or 2016, it seems as if a period of grace has been built into the Canadian age structure. This period can be used as a time of transition, planning and innovation, during which economic and social resources can be gathered in order to provide less to the young, whose diminishing numbers will place less of a burden on society, and more to the old, whose numbers will increase.

CHAPTER 7

IMPLICATIONS OF DEMOGRAPHIC AGING AND UNANSWERED RESEARCH QUESTIONS

Demographic aging in Canada, as we have seen, is not a new phenomenon. Nor is it a process that involves and affects only the older groups in the population. It is inextricably bound to the social structure, the economic system, the political system and to social change. Thus, the implications of demographic aging are wide-reaching, and few Canadian social and economic institutions will remain untouched by it. Meeting the challenges of demographic aging will require considerable understanding of the issues, as well as flexible social planning.

SUMMARY

This book has attempted to clarify the causes of population aging, to expose and refute some of the myths surrounding this phenomenon, and to identify some pertinent research and policy issues. That population aging is due in large part to fertility declines, rather than increases in life expectancy, has been demonstrated. Both fertility decline and population aging are, to a large extent, products of levels of economic development. Thus, population aging can be seen as a byproduct of affluence and economic success. Understanding this relationship is necessary in order to carry out the positive planning for the future that population aging will require.

Our comparison of the chief perspectives used to analyze population aging suggests a need to move beyond demographic description, to a structural explanation of aging, that is, situating the phenomenon within a socioeconomic context. The structural perspective, to the extent that it has been employed so far in a Canadian context, demonstrates that the structural perspective is the way of the future. Reliance on this perspective enables the exploration of the complex interrelationships among social, economic, political and demographic phenomena. Even preliminary evidence from research using a structural perspective shows that the crisis approach to demographic aging is premised on incorrect assumptions.

Our examination of demographic aging in Canada reveals that the population has been aging since before the country came into existence.

Although the process has recently accelerated, aging is not new to Canada. It seems, therefore, that recent concerns about Canada's future in light of demographic aging are somewhat exaggerated. In comparison with other countries, most notably those of Western Europe, Canada is still relatively youthful in demographic terms. More importantly, none of the dire predictions about older countries have come true for those countries that are demographically older than Canada. Again, this calls into question the validity of the alarmism about population aging.

Our examination of the link between population aging and low or no population growth concludes that fears about zero population growth are unfounded. However, these fears have a long history and have contributed to a climate of apprehension about population aging. Our discussion of shifting dependency burdens shows that the issue in an aging society is not so much an increasing dependency burden, as a shifting composition of the burden, which will be increasingly made up of older people instead of children. This will entail a shift from the private to the public sphere for economic and social support. Our examination of the potential effects on mobility chances of an aging society concluded that, although opportunities may be diminished in some cohorts in the future, mobility is as much a function of shifting cohort size and reduced economic opportunity, as the result of population aging. The particular problems faced by older women in Canada at present, while very real and pressing, have tended to create the impression that aging means poverty and dependency. This may not necessarily be the case, as we have seen.

Demographic aging will present complex challenges in the future for Canada's policy-makers. In the economic realm, providing pensions for an increasing number of retirees will provide a challenge, though not an insurmountable one, provided that some redistribution of public monies occurs. The economic problems faced by older women will require a change in policy on pensions for women. The complex issues of economic growth and productivity, including mandatory retirement, will require serious attention in the future from both researchers and policy-makers. In the area of retirement and work, policy concerns involve the growing number of retirees who may transform the meaning of work and leisure, as well as the meaning of volunteer work.

Health issues will have enormous and far-reaching policy implications. The prevention of illness will be an important concern. There is also a need to recognize that illness is socially and economically situated, a need for flexibility in providing chronic care, and a great need for more and better research on the health care requirements of the older population, given that many myths and misconceptions exist. Policy adjustments are necessary in the provision of health care services to an aging population, in order to reduce costs and improve the care provided. The important issue of quality of life for older people, although difficult, must also be addressed by policy-makers as the Canadian population ages.

Housing, social support and education are often neglected areas of policy in an aging society. The changing family in Canada, in combination with the healthier and longer lives of older people, means new needs for familial support and housing. The differential life expectancy of men and women, combined with changing family structure and women's lesser economic independence, means that careful attention should be directed to the needs of widows. Problems involved in moving from a private home to senior citizens' housing must be addressed. Policy issues in providing adequate home care as an alternative to more expensive chronic care should be explored. In the area of educational policy, more is involved than simply transfers from young to old. Consideration must be given to the issue of increased leisure time among the older population and to the possibilities of innovative expansion of educational opportunities to meet their needs.

Lastly, we address the future of demographic aging in Canada. Trends are anticipated in the three major demographic variables (fertility, mortality and migration) and their relative impact on demographic aging in the future is assessed. It is predicted that low fertility is here to stay; that although death rates are not likely to continue to decline, more older people are living longer; and that immigration levels are likely to remain moderate unless policy-makers decide that increasing immigration is the means of "solving" the problems of an aging society. Given these predictions, all based on recent research, it seems that Canada's population will continue to age in the future. There will be small changes in the age composition of the working age population over the next fifty years, but distinct growth in the older population. Overall dependency burdens will not increase dramatically in Canada in the future, but will shift from being composed largely of young people to being composed of older people.

IMPLICATIONS OF DEMOGRAPHIC AGING FOR CANADA

There is no doubt that aging of the Canadian population will create new challenges for policy-makers. It is also clear that the capacity exists to meet these challenges. A panic reaction to an alleged crisis of population aging seems unwarranted and ill-advised. Good decisions can seldom be made in a crisis mode. Realistically, however, it is apparent that some policy-makers will be forced to react to the situation as it develops, rather than with the long-term planning required by demographic aging. This is unfortunate because planning for the shifting needs and requirements of an aging population requires a long-term vision of the future. There is a need now for flexible and rational social planning and problem solving.

Planning, ideally, should entail not simply meeting the growing needs of the older population (although this must be done), but holistic planning for a society experiencing demographic aging. There will no doubt be some who hark back to the "good old days" of high fertility and population growth. There will even be those who will argue that the solution to the demographic "problem" of an aging population rests with increasing the birth rate or levels of immigration or both. Even if these demographic approaches are tried, and even if they work to some extent, the challenges of an aging Canada will still require realistic social planning. The ultimate solutions will not be demographic, but economic and social. Canada's capacity to meet these challenges depends on our willingness to anticipate the future and plan accordingly.

A central issue of the future in an aging society is redistribution of wealth on a relatively small scale. This, no doubt, will not come easily, but neither is it impossible. It could entail a streamlining of the cumbersome and expensive health care system to better meet people's needs and also to reduce costs. It could involve increased taxation to pay for pensions. (This money, however, might be seen as money that would otherwise have been spent on a never-born third child.) There will be transfers of funds from public education to health and social insurance budgets. The blessing of an aging population is that there will actually be fewer people, given a zero or negative population growth rate, and there will be more collective income than in a population composed largely of dependent children.

UNANSWERED QUESTIONS

A great deal is known about demographic aging, yet many questions remain to be answered. A number of these unanswered questions have been noted throughout the book. A few others should be mentioned here. It is hoped that future researchers will be encouraged to explore these areas.

Although much is known about the process, dimensions and dynamics of population aging itself, far less is known about the *links* between demographic aging and socio-economic institutions, structures and systems. In a broad sense, this linkage is an important area of future research on demographic aging. All the specific questions mentioned below essentially fall in this general area.

One unanswered research question is not new at all, but remains to be explored satisfactorily: this is the relationship between personal experience and wider social forces. We are all products of the times in which we live. These times are shaped, among other things, by age structure. This question was addressed by C. Wright Mills' *Sociological Imagination*. It is the crux of what constitutes sociology. Yet it still eludes understanding. With respect to demographic aging, research into intergenerational differences in experience with aging, if framed by the age structures that exist at the different points in time, might provide answers to how personal experience is shaped to some degree by wider forces. For example, research might compare the Depression generation's experiences of retirement with those of the World War II generation. The experiences of the baby boom generation might be contrasted with those of the baby bust generation. This type of research could, if done well, bring together the interactions of generational effects with cohort flow through time.

Another area of potential research would be the changing meaning of old age over time. Demographic research, of course, is predicated on assumptions about when old age begins, as well as assumptions about the social meanings attributed to being in a certain age group. At present, old age is thought to begin at age 65. Should mandatory retirement at age 65 be abolished, this assumption might be called into question. As older people change and become more diversified, it might be that demographers' definitions of dependency would require alteration and increased specificity.

A third unanswered question is actually a cluster of questions, related to the effects of planning. With modern computers it is possible to project many things, including the future effects of alternative plans and policies. For example, what would be the economic and demographic consequences of a rationalized health care system? A projection could be made by anticipating the effects of improved home care, less use of acute care facilities by chronic care patients, less reliance on acute medical intervention where it is not likely to be effective, etc. The relative effects of rationalizing the health care system compared to improved pensions might be assessed. This exercise, of course, would not be straightforward but would involve multiple assumptions about both the present and the future.

Many unanswered questions surround the actual economic needs and activities (consumerism, savings, investments, etc.) of older people. In anticipating the economic consequences of an aging population, many researchers engage in rather sweeping generalizations about the behaviour of older people. For example, economic dependency is often assumed, as is reduced consumer activity. These assumptions need to be backed up by research evidence, rather than taken as given. It may be that the economic activity patterns of older people are very different than we have assumed and will become more so, as you and I arrive at that stage in life. One clue might be derived from the examination of the consumption patterns of the present cohorts of middle-aged Canadians, compared to earlier cohorts.

There is also a need for research to explore the relationship between older people's political power and the demographic definitions of dependency. Dependency suggests helplessness. Older people who are increasingly politically active may be anything but helpless or dependent. The manner in which Canadian pensioners organized to protest the proposal to de-index their pensions in the spring and summer of 1985 provides testimony to their political power. This may be particularly true for women, who tend to outlive men and who also tend to become increasingly politically active as they age.

Finally, there is a need for research to examine the demographic, social and economic implications of abolishing mandatory retirement. It is important, before taking action on mandatory retirement, to understand how this major policy change would affect the various age groups (not only the old), directly or indirectly. This area of research could show the relationships that exist between economic and age structure. It could also address the interactive effects of actions meant to protect the interests of one group in society.

CONCLUSION

The process of aging is complex and multifaceted. Demographic aging is only one component of that process. It is, however, a central component since it reflects our collective experience and provides the broadest social framework in which to plan. It is our hope that this book has added to societal understanding of demographic aging by dispelling some of the misinformation, and by synthesizing research, theory and policy.

BIBLIOGRAPHY

Akers, Donald S.
    1967   "On Measuring the Marriage Squeeze." *Demography* 4(2):907–24.

Auerbach, L., and A. Gerber
    1976   *Perceptions 2: Implications of the Changing Age Structure of the Canadian Population.* Ottawa: Science Council of Canada.

Baker, Paul M.
    1983   "Ageism, Sex and Age: A Factorial Survey Approach." *Canadian Journal on Aging* 2(4):177–84.

Basavarajappa, K. D., and M. V. George
    1981   "The Future Growth and Structure of Canada's Population: Results and Implications of Some Demographic Simulations." *Demographic Trends and Their Impact on the Canadian Labour Market.* (Catalogue No. 8-4200-501). Ottawa: Statistics Canada.

Baum, D.
    1975   *The Final Plateau: The Betrayal of Our Older Citizens.* Toronto: Burns and McEachern.

Bayne, J. R. D.
    1978   "Health and Care Needs of an Aging Population." Paper prepared for the National Symposium on Aging, Ottawa.

Bayne, Ronald, and Blossom Wigdor (eds.)
    1980   *Research Issues in Aging: Report of a Conference.* Hamilton, Ontario: Gerontology Research Council of Ontario.

Beaujot, Roderic, and Kevin McQuillan
    1982   *Growth and Dualism: The Demographic Development of Canadian Society.* Toronto: Gage.

Beaver, Steven E.
    1975   *Demographic Transition Theory Reinterpreted: An Application to Recent Natality Trends in Latin America.* Lexington, Massachusetts: Lexington Books.

Botwinick, J.
    1978   *Aging and Behavior* (2nd ed.). New York: Springer.

Boulet, J. A., and G. Grenier
    1978   "Health Expenditures in Canada and the Impact of Demographic Changes on Future Government Health Insurance Program Expenditures." Discussion Paper No. 123, Economic Council of Canada.

Bourgeois-Pichat, J.
    1978   "Future Outlook for Mortality Decline in the World." *Population Bulletin of the United Nations* No. 11. New York: United Nations.

Bryden, Kenneth
  1974 *Old Age Pensions and Policy-Making in Canada.* Montreal and London: McGill-Queen's University Press.
Butler, Robert
  1969 "Ageism: Another Form of Bigotry." *The Gerontologist* 9(3):243-46.
Calvert, Geoffry N.
  1977 *Pensions and Survival: The Coming Crisis of Money and Retirement.* Toronto: Financial Post.
Canadian Advisory Council on the Status of Women
  1985 *Homemaker Pension.* Ottawa: Canadian Advisory Council on the Status of Women.
Chappell, N. L.
  1982 "The Future Impact of the Changing Status of Women." In Gloria M. Gutman (ed.), *Canada's Changing Age Structure: Implications for the Future.* Burnaby, British Columbia: Simon Fraser University Publications.
Cherlin, Andrew
  1983 "A Sense of History: Recent Research on Aging and the Family." Pp. 5-24 in Matilda White Riley, Beth B. Hess and Kathleen Bond (eds.), *Aging in Society: Selected Reviews of Recent Research.* Hillsdale, New Jersey: Erlbaum.
Clark, Colin
  1967 *History of Population Growth.* London: Macmillan.
Clark, Robert L., and Joseph J. Spengler
  1980 *The Economics of Individual and Population Aging.* Cambridge: Cambridge University Press.
Coale, A. J.
  1956 "The Effects of Changes in Mortality and Fertility on Age Composition." *Millbank Memorial Fund Quarterly* 34:79-114.
Collins, Glen
  1979 "The Good News about 1984." *Psychology Today* (January):34-48.
Collishaw, Neil E.
  1979 "Implications of the Changing Age Structure for Social Policy." Paper presented at conference on the Impact of Changes in Age Distribution, sponsored by the Federation of Canadian Demographers, Montreal, 4-6 October 1979.
Connidis, Ingrid
  1985 "The Service Needs of Older People: Implications for Public Policy." *Canadian Journal on Aging.* 4(1):3-10.
Connidis, Ingrid, and J. Rempel
  1983 "The Living Arrangements of Older Residents: The Role of Gender, Marital Status, Age and Family Size." *Canadian Journal on Aging.* 2(3):91-105.
Crimmins, E. M.
  1983 "Implications of Recent Mortality Trends for the Size and Composition of the Population over 65." *Review of Public Data Use* 11(1):37-44.
Cutler, Neal E., and Robert A. Harootyan
  1982 "Demography of the Aged." Pp. 31-69 in Diana S. Woodruff and

James E. Birren (eds.), *Aging: Scientific Perspectives and Social Issues.* New York: D. Van Nostrand.

Day, Lincoln
- 1972 "The Social Consequences of a Zero Population Growth Rate in the United States." Research paper prepared for the Commission on Population Growth and the American Future.
- 1978 "The Future and Population: What Will a No-Growth Society Be Like?" *Population Reference Bureau Bulletin* 33(3).

Davis, Kingsley, and J. W. Coombs, Jr.
- 1950 "The Sociology of an Aging Population." Pp. 146–70 in Eastern States Health Education Conference, 1949, *The Social and Biological Challenge of Our Aging Population.* New York: Columbia University Press.

Davis, Kingsley, and Pietronella van den Oever
- 1981 "Age Relations and Public Policy in Advanced Industrial Nations." *Population and Development Review* 7(1):1–18.

Deming, M. B., and N. E. Cutler
- 1983 "Demography of the Aged." in Diana S. Woodruff and James E. Birren (eds.), *Aging: Scientific Perspectives and Social Issues.* Monterey, Calif.: Brooks/Cole.

Denton, Frank T., Christine M. Feaver, and Byron G. Spencer
- 1980 *The Future Population and Labour Force of Canada: Projections to the Year 2051.* (A study prepared for the Economic Council of Canada). Ottawa: Minister of Supply and Services.

Denton, Frank T., and Byron G. Spencer
- 1975a "The Demographic Element in the Burden of Government Old Age Pensions." Working Paper No. 75-02. Hamilton, Ontario: McMaster University Economics Department.
- 1975b "Health Care Costs When the Population Changes." *Canadian Journal of Economics* 8:34–48.
- 1976 "The Effects of Demographic Variables on a Pension Scheme: A Macro-Analysis." Working Paper No. 76-01. Hamilton, Ontario: McMaster University, Economics Department.
- 1979 "Some Economic and Demographic Implications of Future Population Change." *Journal of Canadian Studies* 14(1):81–93.
- 1982a "Population Aging, Labour Force Change and Promotion Prospects." Quantitative Studies in Economics and Population, Report No. 30. Hamilton, Ontario: McMaster University.
- 1982b "Population Aging and Future Health-Care Costs in Canada." Quantitative Studies in Economics and Population, Report No. 35. Hamilton, Ontario: McMaster University.
- 1983a "Macroeconomic Aspects of the Transition to Zero Population Growth." Pp. 81–111 in C. Garbacz (ed.), *Economic Resources for the Elderly: Prospects for the Future.* Boulder, Colorado: Westview.
- 1983b "The Sensitivity of Health-Care Costs to Changes in Population Age Structure." Pp. 175–203 in C. Garbacz (ed.), *Economic Resources for the Elderly: Prospects for the Future.* Boulder, Colorado: Westview.
- 1984 "Prospective Changes in the Population and Their Implications for

Government Expenditures." *Quantitative Studies in Economics and Population*, Report No. 98. Hamilton, Ontario: McMaster University.

Dooley, Martin, and Peter Gottschalk
- 1985 "The Increasing Proportion of Men with Low Earnings in the United States." *Demography* 22(1):25-34.

Dulude, L.
- 1978 *Women and Aging: A Report on the Rest of Our Lives*. Ottawa: Advisory Council on the Status of Women.
- 1981 *Pension Reform with Women in Mind*. Ottawa: Advisory Council on the Status of Women.
- 1984 *Love, Marriage and Money*. Ottawa: Canadian Council on the Status of Women.

Easterlin, Richard A.
- 1978 "What Will 1984 Be Like? Socioeconomic Implications of Recent Twists in Age Structure." *Demography* 15(4):397-432.
- 1980 *Birth and Fortune: The Impact of Numbers on Personal Welfare*. New York: Basic Books.

Economic Council of Canada
- 1979 *One in Three: Pensions for Canadians to 2030*. Ottawa: Canadian Government Publishing Centre.

Espenshade, Thomas J., and Rachel Eisenberg Braun
- 1983 "Economic Aspects of an Aging Population and the Material Well-Being of Older Persons." Pp. 25-52 in Matilda White Riley, Beth B. Hess and Kathleen Bond (eds.), *Aging in Society: Selected Reviews of Recent Research*. Hillsdale, New Jersey: Erlbaum.

Foner, Anne, and Karen Schwab
- 1983 "Work and Retirement in a Changing Society." Pp. 71-94 in Matilda White Riley, Beth B. Hess and Kathleen Bond (eds.), *Aging in Society: Selected Reviews of Recent Research*. Hillsdale, New Jersey: Erlbaum.

Foot, David K.
- 1982 *Canada's Population Outlook: Demographic Futures and Economic Challenges*. Toronto: Lorimer.

Freeman, R.
- 1979 "The Effect of Demographic Factors on Age-Earnings Profiles." *Journal of Human Resources* 14:289-318.

Friedlander, Dov, and Ruth Klinov-Malul
- 1980 "Aging of Populations, Dependency and Economic Burden in Developed Countries." *Canadian Studies in Population* 7:49-56.

Garfield, Eugene
- 1984 "Social Gerontology. Part 2. Demography. The Effects of an Aging Population on Society." *Current Contents* (May) 22:3-13.

Gee, Ellen
- 1981 "Population." Chapter 10 in R. Hagedorn (ed.), *Essentials of Sociology*. Toronto: Holt, Rinehart and Winston.
- 1982 "Discussion of John F. Myles' 'Social Implications of a Changing Age Structure'." Pp. 59-66 in Gloria M. Gutman (ed.), *Canada's Changing Age Structure: Implications for the Future*. Burnaby, British Columbia: Simon Fraser University Publications.

George, M. V., and A. Romaniuc
- 1983 "Emerging Major Demographic Issues of the 1980's and Their Implications for Planning and Policy-Making." Paper presented to Canadian Population Society, Vancouver, B.C.

Gnanasekaren, K. S.
- 1975 *Mortality Trends in Projections for Canada and the Provinces, 1950–1986.* Technical Report on Population Projections for Canada and the Provinces, 1972–2001. (Catalogue No. 81-516). Ottawa: Statistics Canada.

Graebner, William
- 1980 *A History of Retirement.* New Haven: Yale University Press.

Grindstaff, Carl
- 1975 "The Baby Bust: Changes in Fertility Patterns in Canada." *Canadian Studies in Population* 2:15–22.
- 1984 "Catching Up: The Fertility of Women Over 30 Years of Age, Canada in the 1970's and 1980's." *Canadian Studies in Population* 11(2):95–110.
- 1985 "The Baby Bust Revisited: Canada's Continuing Pattern of Low Fertility." *Canadian Studies in Population* 12(1):103-10.

Gutman, Gloria
- 1980 "The Elderly at Home and in Retirement Housing." Pp. 189–200 in Victor W. Marshall (ed.), *Aging in Canada: Social Perspectives.* Don Mills, Ontario: Fitzhenry and Whiteside.

Gutman, Gloria M. (ed.)
- 1982 *Canada's Changing Age Structure: Implications for the Future.* Burnaby, British Columbia: Simon Fraser University Publications.

Havens, B.
- 1982 "Population Projections: Certainties and Uncertainties." In Gloria M. Gutman (ed.), *Canada's Changing Age Structure: Implications for the Future.* Burnaby, British Columbia: Simon Fraser University Publications.

Hawkins, Freda
- 1972 *Canada and Immigration: Public Policy and Public Concern.* Montreal: McGill-Queen's University Press.
- 1985 "Towards a Population Policy for Canada: Past and Present Policy Development in the Field of Canadian Immigration and Population." Paper presented at the meetings of the Canadian Population Society, Montreal, May–June 1985.

Health and Welfare Canada
- 1982 *Canadian Governmental Report on Aging.* Ottawa: Minister of Supply and Services.
- 1983 *Fact Book on Aging in Canada.* Ottawa: Minister of Supply and Services.

Hermalin, A. I.
- 1966 "The Effects of Changes in Mortality Rates on Population Growth and Age Distribution in the United States." *Millbank Memorial Fund Quarterly* 44:451–69.

Herzog, John P.
- 1982 "Aging, Pensions and Demographic Change." Pp. 125–43 in Gloria M.

Gutman (ed.), *Canada's Changing Age Structure: Implications for the Future*. Burnaby, British Columbia: Simon Fraser University Publications.

Jackson, Jacquelyn J.
   1980 *Minorities and Aging*. Belmont, California: Wadsworth.

Kerschner, Paul A., and Ira S. Hirschfield
   1982 "Public Policy and Aging: Analytical Approaches." Pp. 352–73 in Diana S. Woodruff and James E. Birren (eds.), *Aging: Scientific Perspectives and Social Issues*. New York: D. Van Nostrand Co.

Keyfitz, Nathan
   1972 "On Future Population." *Journal of the American Statistical Association* 67(338):347–63.
   1973 "Individual Mobility in a Stationary Population." *Population Studies* 27(2):335–52.
   1980 "Why Social Security is in Trouble." *The Public Interest* 58:102–19.

Kii, T.
   1982 "A New Index for Measuring Demographic Aging." *The Gerontologist* 22(4):438–42.

Lalonde, Marc
   1978 *A New Perspective on the Health of Canadians*. Ottawa: Information Canada.

Lefebre, L. A., Z. Zsigmond, and M. S. Devereux
   1979 *A Prognosis for Hospitals*. (Catalogue No. 83-520). Ottawa: Statistics Canada Data.

Lipovenko, Dorothy
   1985 "Immigration Rules Eased for Retired in Effort to Attract Foreign Wealth." *The Globe and Mail*, 2 August 1985, p. 1.

Longino, C.
   1982 "Symposium: Population Research for Planning and Practice." *The Gerontologist* 22(2/1982):142–69.

MacLean, Michael J.
   1983 "Differences between Adjustment and Enjoyment of Retirement." *Canadian Journal on Aging* 2(1):3–8.

Macleod, Betty
   1979 "The Female Labour Force in an Aging Society." Paper presented at conference on the Impact of Changes in Age Distribution, sponsored by the Federation of Canadian Demographers. Montreal, 4–6 October 1979.

Maddox, G. L.
   1982 "Aging People and Aging Populations: A Framework for Decision-Making." Pp. 19–30 in H. Thomae and G. L. Maddox (eds.), *New Perspectives on Old Age*. New York: Springer.

Maddox, G. L., and J. Wiley
   1976 "Scope, Concepts and Methods in the Study of Aging." In R. Binstock and E. Shanas (eds.), *The Handbook of Aging and the Social Sciences*. New York: Van Nostrand Reinhold.

Madigan, Francis C.
   1968 "Are Sex Mortality Differences Biologically Caused?" Pp. 152–63 in Charles B. Nam (ed.), *Population and Society*. New York: Houghton Mifflin.

Marshall, Victor W. (ed.)
   1980   *Aging in Canada: Social Perspectives.* Don Mills, Ontario: Fitzhenry and Whiteside.

Martin, James K.
   1982   "Social Policy Concerns Related to Retirement: Implications for Research." Pp. 145–202 in Gloria M. Gutman (ed.), *Canada's Changing Age Structure: Implications for the Future.* Burnaby, British Columbia: Simon Fraser University Publications.

Matthews, Anne Martin, Joseph B. Tindale and Joan E. Norris
   1984   "The Facts on Aging Quiz: A Canadian Validation and Cross-Cultural Comparison." *Canadian Journal on Aging* 3(4):165–74.

McDaniel, Susan A.
   1984a   "Explaining Canadian Fertility: Some Remaining Challenges." *Canadian Studies in Population* 11(1):1–16.
   1984b   "Family Size Expectations among Selected Edmonton Women: Three Explanatory Frameworks Compared." *Canadian Review of Sociology and Anthropology* 21(1):75–91.
   1985   "Shifting Opportunities in Canada's Aging Society: Contrasting Prospects for Men and for Women." Paper prepared for Canadian Population Society Meetings, Montreal, 1985.

McDaniel, Susan A. and Ben Agger
   1982   "Population as a Social Problem." Chapter 8 in Susan A. McDaniel and Ben Agger, *Social Problems Through Conflict and Order.* Don Mills, Ontario: Addison-Wesley.

McDaniel, Susan A. and Benson Morah
   1975   *Aging in Alberta: Determinants and Projections.* Alberta Series Report No. 6, Population Research Laboratory, University of Alberta, Edmonton, Alberta.

McLean, Linda
   1977   "The Displacement of Youth and the Revolution of Rising Expectations." Working Paper. Ottawa: Health and Welfare Canada.

McPherson, Barry D.
   1983   *Aging as a Social Process: An Introduction to Individual and Population Aging.* Toronto: Butterworths.

Miller, D.
   1981   "The 'Sandwich Generation': Adult Children of the Aging." *Social Work* 26(5):419–23.

Myers, George
   1982   "The Aging Populations." In Robert Binstock, Wing-Sun Chow and James N. Schultz (eds.), *International Perspectives on Aging: Population Challenges.* New York: United Nations Fund for Population Activities.

Myles, John F.
   1980   "The Aged, the State and the Structure of Inequality." Pp. 317–42 in J. Harp and J. Hofley (eds.), *Structured Inequality in Canada.* Toronto: Prentice-Hall.
   1982   "Social Implications of Canada's Changing Age Structure." Pp. 33–58 in Gloria M. Gutman (ed.), *Canada's Changing Age Structure: Implications for the Future.* Burnaby, British Columbia: Simon Fraser University Publications.

1984   *Old Age in the Welfare State: The Political Economy of Public Pensions.* Toronto: Little, Brown.

Myles, John F. and Monica Boyd
    1982   "Population Aging and the Elderly." Pp. 258-85 in D. Forcese and Stephen Richer (eds.), *Social Issues: Sociological Views of Canada.* Scarborough, Ontario: Prentice-Hall.

National Advisory Committee on Aging
    1983   *Moving Ahead with Aging in Canada.* Ottawa: National Advisory Committee on Aging.

Neugarten, Bernice L.
    1974   "Age Groups in American Society and the Rise of the Young Old." Pp. 187-98 in F. R. Eisele (ed.), *Political Consequences of Aging.* The Annals of the American Academy of Political and Social Science, No. 415.

Northcott, Herbert C.
    1984   "The Aging of Canada's Population: An Update from the 1981 Census." *Canadian Studies in Population* 11(1):29-46.
    1984   "The Interprovincial Migration of Canada's Elderly." *Canadian Journal on Aging* 3(1):3-22.
    1984   "Widowhood and Remarriage Trends in Canada: 1956-1981." *Canadian Journal on Aging* 3(2):63-77.

Notestein, F. W., I. B. Taeuber, C. Kirk, A. J. Coale, and L. K. Kiser
    1944   *The Future Population of Europe and the Soviet Union.* Geneva: League of Nations.

OCUFA Forum. (Ontario Confederation of University Faculty Associations)
    1985   Vol. 4(18) March.

Overbeek, Johannes
    1980   *Population and Canadian Society.* Toronto: Butterworths.

Palmore, E., and K. Manton
    1974   "Modernization and the Status of the Aged: International Correlations." *Journal of Gerontology* 29:205-10.

Patterson, Keith
    1980   "Some Economic Implications of the Projected Age Structure of Canada: Comments." *Canadian Public Policy* 6(3):542-44.

Phillips, P., and E. Phillips
    1983   *Women and Work.* Toronto: Lorimer.

Phillipson, Chris
    1982   *Capitalism and the Construction of Old Age.* London: Macmillan.

Powell, Brian J., and James K. Martin
    1980   "Economic Implications of Canada's Aging Society." Pp. 204-14 in Victor W. Marshall (ed.), *Aging in Canada: Social Perspectives.* Don Mills, Ontario: Fitzhenry and Whiteside.

Ridler, Neil B.
    1979   "Some Economic Implications of the Projected Age Structure of Canada." *Canadian Public Policy* 5(4):533-41.

Riley, Matilda White, and Kathleen Bond
    1983   "Beyond Ageism: Postponing the Onset of Disability." Pp. 243-52 in Matilda White Riley, Beth B. Hess and Kathleen Bond (eds.), *Aging in*

Society: Selected Reviews of Recent Research. Hillsdale, New Jersey: Erlbaum.

Roadburg, Alan
   1985   *Aging: Retirement, Leisure and Work in Canada*. Toronto: Methuen.

Romaniuc, A.
   1973   "Potentials for Population Growth in Canada: A Long Term Projection." In *A Population Policy for Canada?* Toronto: Conservation Council of Ontario & The Family Planning Federation of Canada.

Rossett, E.
   1964   *Aging Process of Population*. New York: Pergamon Press.

Russell, L. B.
   1981   "An Aging Population and the Use of Medical Care." *Medical Care* 19 (June):633-43.

Ryder, Norman
   1975   "Notes on Stationary Populations." *Population Index* 41:3-28.

Sauvy, A.
   1948   "Social and Economic Consequences of the Aging of Western European Populations." *Population Studies* 2(1):115-24.

Schrank, Harris T., and Joan M. Waring
   1983   "Aging and Work Organizations." Pp. 53-70 in Matilda White Riley, Beth B. Hess and Kathleen Bond (eds.), *Aging in Society: Selected Reviews of Recent Research*. Hillsdale, New Jersey: Erlbaum.

Serow, William J., and Thomas J. Espenshade
   1978   *The Economic Consequences of Slowing Population Growth*. New York: Academic Press.

Shryrock, H. S., and J. S. Siegel
   1975   *The Methods and Materials of Demography*. Washington, D.C.: Bureau of the Census.

Siegel, J. S.
   1980   "On the Demography of Aging." *Demography* 17:345-64.
   1981   "Demographic Background for International Gerontological Studies." *Journal of Gerontology* 36(1):93-102.

Siegel, J. S., and Sally L. Hoover
   1982   "Demographic Aspects of the Health of the Elderly to the Year 2000 and Beyond." *World Health Statistics Quarterly* 35:133-202.

Spencer, Byron G., and Frank T. Denton
   1983   "Population Aging and Future Health Costs in Canada." *Canadian Public Policy* 9(2).
   1984   "The Time Path of the Economy as the Population Moves Towards a Stationary State." In G. Steinman (ed.), *Economic Consequences of Population Change in Industrialized Countries*. New York: Springer-Verlag.

Spengler, Joseph J.
   1978   *Facing Zero Population Growth: Reactions and Interpretations, Past and Present*. Durham, N.C.: Duke University Press.

Statistics Canada
   1976   *1971 Census of Canada. Profile Studies: The Age Structure of Canada's Population*. Volume V, Part 1.

1978 *Canada's Elderly*. Ottawa: Minister of Supply and Services.
1978 *Prognosis for Hospitals: The Effects of Population Change on the Need for Hospital Space 1967–2031*. Health Division. Ottawa: Minister of Supply and Services.
1982 *Pension Plans in Canada 1980* (Catalogue No. 74-401). Ottawa: Minister of Supply and Services.
1982 *1981 Census of Canada*. (Catalogue No. 92-901). Ottawa: Minister of Supply and Services.
1984a *Current Demographic Analysis, Report on the Demographic Situation in Canada in 1983*. Prepared by Jean Dumas. (Catalogue No. 91-209E Annual). Ottawa: Minister of Supply and Services.
1984b *Current Demographic Analysis, Fertility in Canada: From Baby Boom to Baby Bust*. Written by A. Romaniuc. (Catalogue No. 91-524E Occasional). Ottawa: Minister of Supply and Services.
1984c *The Elderly in Canada*. (Catalogue No. 99-932). Ottawa: Minister of Supply and Services.
1984d *Highlights: 1981 Census of Canada*. (Catalogue No. 92-X-535-E). Ottawa: Minister of Supply and Services.
1984e *Life Tables, Canada and Provinces*. (Catalogue No. 84-532). Ottawa: Minister of Supply and Services.
1985 *Population Projections for Canada, Provinces and Territories, 1984–2006*. (Catalogue No. 91-520). Ottawa: Minister of Supply and Services.

Steinman, Gunter (ed.)
1984 *Economic Consequences of Population Change in Industrialized Countries*. New York: Springer-Verlag.

Stone, Leroy O., and Susan Fletcher
1980 *A Profile of Canada's Older Population*. Montreal: Institute for Research on Public Policy.
1981 *Aspects of Population Aging in Canada: A Chartbook*. Ottawa: Minister of Supply and Services.

Stone, Leroy O., and Michael J. MacLean
1979 *Future Income Prospects for Canada's Senior Citizens*. Montreal: Institute for Research on Public Policy.

Stone, Leroy, and Claude Marceau
1977 *Canadian Population Trends and Public Policy Through the 1980's*. Montreal and London: Institute for Research on Public Policy and McGill-Queen's University Press.

Taylor, C. E.
1978 *Population Policy Development in Canada, 1970–1977: The Role of Interest Groups*. Toronto: University of Toronto Geography Department.

Thomae, Hans, and George L. Maddox (eds.)
1982 *New Perspectives on Old Age: A Message to Decision-Makers*. New York: Springer.

Thomas, W. I.
1923 *The Unadjusted Girl*. Boston: Little, Brown.

Thornton, James E.
1983 "Issues Affecting Geronotology Education and Manpower Needs in Population Aging." *Canadian Journal on Aging* 2(3):123-62.

Uhlenberg, Peter
    1979   "Demographic Change and Problems of the Aged." Pp. 153–66 in Matilda White Riley (ed.), *Aging from Birth to Death: Interdisciplinary Perspectives*, AAAS Selected Symposium Series No. 30. Boulder, Colorado: Westview Press.

United Nations
    1954   "The Cause of the Aging of Populations: Declining Mortality or Declining Fertility?" *Population Bulletin of the United Nations* 4:30–38.
    1973   *The Determinants and Consequences of Population Trends*. Population Studies No. 50. New York: United Nations.
    1984   *Demographic Yearbook, 1982*. New York: United Nations.

United States Commission on Population Growth and the American Future
    1972   *Population and the American Future, Final Report*. Washington, D.C.: Government Printing Office.

Veevers, Jean E.
    1981   "Demographic Aspects of Vital Statistics: Fertility. A Statistical Workshop held in Ottawa, 12–13 March 1981." Unpublished manuscript.

Wander, Hilda
    1978   "ZPG Now: The Lesson from Europe." Pp. 41–69 in Thomas Espenshade and William Serow (eds.), *The Economic Consequences of Slowing Population Growth*. New York: Academic Press.

Weitz, Harvy
    1976   "Income Maintenance for the Elderly in Canada." Pp. 135–49 in *Papers from the Economics of Aging: Toward 2001*. Detroit, Michigan: The Institute of Gerontology, The University of Michigan — Wayne State University.

Wigdor, B. T.
    1978   "Implications of the Demographic Changes in the Canadian Population over the Next 25 Years." Paper presented at the National Symposium on Aging, Ottawa.

Wilkins, Russell
    1983   "The Burden of Ill-Health in Canada: Socio-economic Inequalities in the Healthfulness of Life." Unpublished revised version of a paper presented at the Special Seminar Series on Population and Health Care, McMaster University, Faculty of Health Sciences, Hamilton, Ontario.

Wilkins, Russell, and Owen Adams
    1983   "Health Expectancy in Canada, Late 1970's: Demographic, Regional and Social Dimensions." *American Journal of Public Health* 73(9): 1073–80.

Wilson, S. J.
    1982   *Women, the Family and the Economy*. Toronto: McGraw-Hill Ryerson.

INDEX

A

Adams, 14, 15
age-specific mortality, 198
ageism, 56, 183, 184
Akers, 61
alarmism (etc.), 19, 26, 31, 35, 39, 53, 54, 55, 73, 92, 116
attitudes, 21, 27, 50, 51, 52, 53, 56, 77, 78, 83, 86, 88

B

baby boomers (etc.), 3, 37, 49, 56, 60, 61, 63, 76, 77, 78, 90, 93, 94, 96, 97, 102, 103, 104, 105, 114, 118
baby bust, 61, 68, 96, 102, 114, 118
Bayne, 83
Beaujot, 46, 51, 94, 101, 102
Beaver, 8
Bond, 83
Boyd, 3
Butler, 56

C

Calvert, 54, 55, 68, 69, 70
Canada Health Survey, 14, 81, 82
Canada Pension Plan, 64, 71, 72
Canada Sickness Survey, 82
Canadian Advisory Council on Status of Women, 64, 72, 73
Canadian Population Society, 62
Charter of Rights, 74, 75
Chronic Care, 79, 81, 82, 83, 116, 117, 119
Clark, C., 46

Coale, 11
cohort flow, 3, 4, 5, 17, 111, 119
Collins, 4
composition, 10, 23, 53, 68, 110, 116, 117
Connidis, 84, 87
creativity, 56, 58, 66
crisis, 25, 26, 27, 28, 55, 115, 117

D

Davis, 25, 53, 54
Day, 51
demographic determinism, 25, 26, 28
Denton, 55, 59, 62, 64, 69, 85, 94, 98, 100, 101, 112
dependence, 10, 11, 12, 26, 27, 34, 37, 40, 41, 50, 53, 54, 55, 56, 57, 58, 59, 63, 64, 65, 66, 68, 69, 70, 73, 79, 87, 89, 113, 114, 116, 117, 118, 119
dependency ratio, 11, 24, 25, 55, 111, 112, 113
disability-free life expectancy, 14, 85
Dooley, 59
Dulude, 41, 64, 65, 73

E

Easterlin, 4, 12, 13, 25, 59, 60, 62
Economic Council of Canada, 57
Elder Hostel, 191

F

Feaver, 64, 94, 98, 100, 101, 112
fertility, 4, 6, 8, 9, 11, 12, 13, 14,

fertility—*cont.*
  15, 17, 22, 23, 25, 35, 37, 45,
  46, 49, 50, 52, 53, 69, 87, 91,
  93, 94, 96, 97, 98, 101, 102, 103,
  104, 105, 106, 107, 113, 115, 117
Fletcher, 69, 70, 71, 81, 84, 85, 88, 89
Foner, 75
Foot, 36, 37, 55, 69, 70, 90, 91, 98, 99
Freeman, 59
Friedlander, 11, 50
functionalism, 27

G

Gee, 6, 8, 37, 97
generation gap, 25
gerontology, 22, 85, 92
Globe & Mail, 75
Gottschalk, 59
Graebner, 56
granny flat, 89
Grey Panthers, 77
Grindstaff, 37, 52, 96, 97
Guaranteed Income Supplement, 71
Gutman, 88, 89, 90

H

Havens, 105
Hawkins, 67, 101
Health & Welfare Canada, 11, 29, 36,
  41, 42, 43, 63, 71, 72, 73, 81, 82,
  84, 85, 87, 88, 89, 90, 91, 100
health care, 5, 11, 22, 25, 26, 27, 43,
  48, 51, 57, 58, 59, 60, 65, 68, 69,
  79, 80, 81, 82, 83, 84, 85, 86, 90,
  116, 118, 119
health promotion, 84
Hermalin, 11
Herzog, 70
home care, 81, 83, 86, 88, 117, 119
homemakers, 64, 71, 72
hospices, 84
housing, 25, 65, 67, 80, 86, 88, 89, 90, 92, 117

I

immigration, 1, 6, 35, 37, 42, 62, 67,
  68, 70, 90, 99, 100, 101, 102,
  103, 104, 105, 106, 111, 117, 118
infant mortality, 99
institutional health care, 82, 84
institutionalization, 82, 86, 87, 90

J

Jackson, 14

K

Keyfitz, 62
Keynes, 48
Kii, 11, 12, 15
Klinov-Malul, 11, 50

L

Lalonde, 80
life chances, 4, 61
life cycles, 2, 63
life expectancy, 5, 9, 14, 15, 30, 31,
  45, 47, 49, 50, 62, 64, 73, 77, 86,
  87, 98, 99, 105, 115, 117
life insurance, 74
life span, 6, 47, 49
life table, 198
Lipovenko, 70
long-term care, 82, 84
longevity, 50, 187

M

MacLean, 76, 84
Madigan, 31
Malthus, 22, 26
mandatory retirement, 74, 75, 79, 116, 119
Manton, 27
Marceau, 67, 70

Marx, 22, 27
McDaniel, 52, 62
McPherson, 12, 57, 75, 77, 78, 92
McQuillan, 46, 51, 94, 101, 102
mean age, 5
median age, 9, 13, 36, 37, 58, 101, 105
medical care, 5
migration, 23, 90, 91, 99, 100, 111, 117
Mills, 118
mobility, 4, 12, 13, 45, 47, 53, 59, 60, 61, 62, 63, 74, 75, 78, 86, 87, 116
mortality, 5, 9, 11, 12, 15, 23, 35, 45, 46, 47, 49, 50, 51, 52, 57, 71, 82, 86, 93, 98, 99, 101, 102, 104, 105, 106, 117
Mulroney, 70
Myles, 3, 24, 27, 55, 68, 69, 70, 72

N

native children, 81
native people, 43
Neugarten, 11
Northcott, 87, 111
Notestein, 56
nurse-practitioners, 85

O

OCUFA forum, 73
old age dependency ratio, 11, 34, 35, 38, 54, 113
old age dependency, 35, 54, 55
old age security, 71, 72
Osler, 56
Overbeek, 53

P

Palmore, 27
Patterson, 54
pension, 5, 11, 25, 26, 27, 31, 41, 48, 50, 51, 52, 54, 55, 58, 59, 60, 64, 65, 68, 69, 70, 71, 72, 73, 74, 77, 78, 79, 84, 87, 88, 89, 90, 92, 116, 118, 119
Phillips, E., 64, 72
Phillips, P., 64, 72
Phillipson, 24
population pyramid, 6, 8, 15, 45, 50, 102, 103, 104, 107, 110
prediction, 1, 4, 23, 55, 85, 104, 105
productivity, 27, 34, 53, 54, 55, 56, 57, 58, 68, 73, 74, 75, 85, 116
projections, 1, 6, 8, 22, 23, 24, 34, 38, 55, 91, 93, 104, 105, 111, 112, 113, 119

Q

quality of later life, 48
quality of life, 14, 63, 80, 85, 86, 116
Quebec Pension Plan, 71, 72

R

Rempel, 87
retirement, 1, 10, 12, 49, 59, 64, 65, 67, 70, 72, 74, 75, 76, 77, 78, 82, 87, 89, 90, 92, 102, 103, 104, 116
reverse mortgages, 189
Ridler, 54, 55
Riley, 183
Rossett, 12, 13
Ryder, 13, 14

S

Sauvy, 57
Schwab, 76
senility, 82
sex ratio, 40, 41, 63, 110
Shryrock, 13
Siegel, 13, 29
simulation, 23, 69, 84, 85
Spencer, 55, 59, 62, 64, 69, 85, 94, 98, 100, 101, 112

Spengler, 46, 48, 62
Statistics Canada, 3, 6, 13, 23, 64, 72, 94, 96, 97, 98, 99, 100, 101, 103, 104, 105, 106, 111
Stone, 67, 69, 70, 71, 81, 84, 85, 88, 89

T

Taylor, 101
Thomas, 51
Thornton, 192
total dependency, 37, 38, 54, 113
total dependency ratio, 37, 38, 39, 55, 112, 113

U

United Nations, 3, 9, 11, 29

V

van den Oever, 25, 53, 54
volunteer, 79
volunteer work, 79, 116

W

Wander, 69
Weitz, 71
widow, 41, 63, 64, 71, 87, 88, 117
widower, 87
Wigdor, 83
Wilkins, 14, 15, 85, 86
Wilson, 72, 73, 78
women, 1, 14, 25, 26, 31, 40, 41, 45, 52, 57, 58, 61, 62, 63, 64, 65, 68, 70, 71, 72, 73, 74, 77, 78, 79, 81, 83, 87, 88, 93, 96, 98, 99, 103, 106, 110, 116, 117, 119
women's movement, 13

Y

youth dependency, 55
youth dependency ratio, 11, 52

Z

zero population growth, 9, 11, 45, 46, 47, 48, 49, 51, 52, 53, 54, 55, 96, 103, 116, 118